**HOW TO RESUME AFTER**

A true story behind th

# to.be.
# con
# tinued

to.be continued
from dis.con.tinued

# Fernando E. Franco Sr.

ISBN 978-0-578-69663-8 (paperback)
ISBN 978-0-578-69664-5 (digital)

For more information visit, https://www.onlinechurchgrowthmaterial.com/

*to.be.continued*

Printed in the United States of America Published by Franco Publishing Company

Cover design by Richell Balansag
Line Editing by Amos at Christian Book Editing Omar Lopez Jr.
Copy Editing by Omar Lopez Jr.
Interior Design by Marvin Lui
Cover Photo of Fernando E. Franco Sr. taken by Genji at Ooka Photography

Religion, motivational, leadership, spiritual

Follow Fernando E. Franco Sr.

Twitter @pastorfernie | Instagram @pastorfernie | Facebook @Fernie Franco Sr.|
YouTube @Fernie Franco | @ FERNIE FRANCO The Podcast

# DEDICATION

(Dad Mondy and mom Charlotte.)

To my father, the late **Armondo "Mondy" Franco**. You died too soon for us all. I know that we had to let you go because your tenacity would have fought another day for your family if we had allowed you. It would have been very selfish of me, my mom, brother, sister, and the rest of our family to keep you a day longer in your condition. Dad, you deserved heaven, and it was your time for you to get it!

I love you and dedicated this book to you, Dad—my father that I give honor to.

# CONTENTS

# ACKNOWLEDGMENTS

(My immediate family)

To my mother-in-law, Rosie Gauna (RIP).
You raised ten children that honored and loved you.
Before you passed, you spoke into your daughter's
(Veronica) life and cheered her on with the words,
"Man didn't call you and Fernando, God did."
May you rest in paradise, good and faithful servant.

To my immediate family,
You have witnessed it all. You have supported me.
You have been patient with me. You have loved me
unconditionally. I love you so much, Veronica Franco,
Fernand Franco Jr., Destiny Franco, Hannah Franco,
Angel Borjas Jr., and my son, Nehemiah Hunter Franco (RIP).

To the Thrive Mentorship House,
We live together. We celebrate together. We cry together.
We are transforming together. We are family, and you are miracles
in God's making. Thank you for changing every day.
I can't wait to see the finished product in your lives.

To CityView Worship Church,
We have come a very long way in just 2 ½ short years.
We are destined for great and mighty things in Oxnard,
California, and across the globe. Remain available, willing,
and ready. God wants to use us for His Glory and the Kingdom.
A very special thank you to all the licensed ministers at CVW.

To all of you reading this book,
Somehow this book reached you. Whether you purchased
it or it was given or borrowed, I acknowledge you
for taking the time to read. I pray it transforms your life.

To my mother Charlotte, sister Monica, and brother Mando.
I love you all very much. In my eyes,
blood is thicker than any other fluid on planet earth.

# INTRODUCTION

**Con.tin.ued (Definition)** *"…to remain in existence or operation: Carry on with, to recommence or resume after interruption:*

So much has happened since the release of *dis.con.tinued*, my first book. Unfortunately, my good friend and confidant, Pete Salgado, who forwarded *dis.con.tinued,* lost his life the year after the book's release date, due to an illness. His family is mourning as well as myself and the rest of his friends and family.

My prayer behind the entire book project was that "if the book could just help one person from ending their life, then I would be completely fulfilled with all the efforts that were invested into the book." Since the release of *dis.con.tinued,* so many have responded with reports on how the book saved, transformed, and gave them a second chance at life.

*dis.con.tinued* was published on June 28, 2019. It was intentionally published that day because the year 1987, June 28th, I accepted Jesus Christ into my heart. I have been fortunate enough to have traveled outside the United States of America and to Europe, promoting the book with many being touched by the hope found in *dis.con.tinued.*

Immediately after the published date, Amazon ranked the book #1 in their "new release categories" in Christian Church growth and Suicide.

If you had the chance to read my first book, *dis.con.tinued*, you know how close I came to ending my life as a pastor. Pastors aren't immune to the rising suicide rates. In fact, more than half of pastors have counseled people who were later diagnosed with mental illness (59 percent), and about a quarter say they've experienced some type of mental illness themselves (23 percent). <u>According</u> to LifeWay, 12 percent have been diagnosed with a mental health condition.

Being a pastor is a dangerous job!

Jesus said: *The good shepherd lays down his life for the sheep* (John 10:11; New International Version). I know He is referring to Himself as the good shepherd. However, He used this analogy as what the shepherd does for the sheep.

It has only been by the grace of God, and I'm also alive today because of my wife, family, and friends.

I now present you with my second book, *to.be.continued.*

In the epilogue of my first book, I mentioned: *As long as we are living with humans, we are always at the chance of being **dis.con.tinued**. We are not dealing with **products** or **paper**, but with **people**. Products and paper are made up of materials; people of all races and colors are made up of feelings. Real people with real feelings are always free to feel what they want to feel and judge who they want to judge. Many times, we are the ones being judged.*

*God gave us all our individual capacity of feelings. And because people have that right, we are always in the danger of being labeled as **dis.con. tinued**.*

*Remember this; if we would just remove the word **dis** from **continued**, and add the words **to** & **be**, then we would go from **dis.con.tinued** – **to.be.continued.***

So, in *to.be.continued*, allow me to help you discover **HOW TO RESUME AFTER LIFE'S BIGGEST INTERRUPTIONS.** We all have them! No one is exempt. There is a huge difference in my first book from this book.

In my first book, I thought life was finished. In this book, I'll help you to carry on your life after the pause.

It's time to read this book. Your pause has come to an end—press play. Let us get going and get back at doing life and loving it!

We are officially going **TO.BE.CONTINUED** from DIS.CON.TINUED.

# CHAPTER ONE

# BUT IT STILL HURTS!

*"My mama always said, 'Life was like a box of chocolates. You never know what you're gonna get."*

—*Forrest Gump*

*I say: "Life is like a box full of darkness. This too is a gift."*

—*Fernando E. Franco Sr.*

**B**ut it still hurts! When God created the world, darkness was part of it—"And God called the light **Day**, and the darkness he called **Night**." This is a factual reality. We all have experienced hurt in some way or another—physically, emotionally or perhaps, relationally. Some can wipe the dust off within the same hour hurtful things occurred while others carry it with them for a lifetime. This all depends on the pain barrier of each person. I don't know who you are, but let's just say you fall into the latter.

Bumps, bruises, and broken bones are common in every sport. The most entertaining and highest in television ratings are contact sports that involve highly competitive athletes who'll risk their lives just to win. Often, at a press conference between two fighters, you'll hear the expression from one or the other, "I'm going to rearrange his face!"

I have found that getting hurt in this thing that we call life will not only rearrange a face but also rearrange how close you allow someone within your reach. There are so many people who want to help us, but because our face has been rearranged, so has the limitation of help that is rearranged with it.

I've always loved contact sports. Maybe because at age eleven, I began competing in full contact Karate. One day, my daughter and I were at the Staples Center in Los Angeles, California. We had the honor of meeting the MMA fighter, "The California Kid," Uriah Faber that day. The moment of meeting and greeting was very special and memorable. I was immediately thrown into reminiscing the fight between him and Mike Brown. Admittedly, a broken hand is an occupational hazard for anyone who calls face-punching their profession. It happens a lot. It comes with the territory. However, breaking not one but two hands—*both hands*—is something different altogether. A double hand-break is akin to a soccer player losing his legs during the 90-minute game, leaving him only with the use of his head. It removes two vital components used to pursue victory, and worse, strips a fighter of their defense and ability to protect themselves adequately.

Urijah Faber knows the feeling only too well. He cracked Mike Brown with a roundhouse right in the opening round of their fight in June 2009, which broke two of the bones in his right hand. He then somehow managed to do something similar to his left hand in round three, having resorted to chucking wild uppercuts at Brown, one of which glanced off his elbow. "I couldn't even make a fist after that first round," he said, "I was faking that my hand was okay even though it was throbbing. I proceeded to throw lefts and kicks and knees. Everything but that right hand. Once I got through that second round, I knew I could do this."

But then came the uppercut in round three. Now, his thumb was dislocated—meaning both hands were out of use. "I literally had no hands at all," he said. "I was letting him get in close and throwing elbows and faking takedowns and going for knees. I ended up almost getting a submission in the fifth round. I lost a decision but gained a lot of respect and a lot of knowledge about myself."

## HURT ISN'T ALWAYS A NEGATIVE

Pain is one way our body communicates to us that something is wrong. At times, the hurt is a constant reminder of our humanity. Paul the Apostle complained of the thorn in his flesh. It reminded him that he was not above any other human being. Despite that, **it still hurts!** Although such circumstances may be a

**PAIN IS ONE WAY OUR BODY COMMUNICATES TO US THAT SOMETHING IS WRONG.**

good thing for the meantime, if God decides to take it away, He will. However, His will may just be to keep it there for a lifetime. I don't know God's will for your life; all I do is pray God's will for people's life. I'm not the author and the finisher. I'm just an author of this

3

book, but I do know one thing from a personal point of view, God sometimes allows hurt to be short, long, or be for a lifetime.

As "The California Kid," Urijah Faber said after his bout while fighting hurt, "I lost a decision but gained a lot of respect and a lot of knowledge about myself."

We'll be surprised how much we can learn about ourselves in the dark. After all, in the dark moments of our lives, most of the time, all we can see is ourselves in a dark room.

We may have been hurt many times, and just like Forrest Gump said in the opening paragraph of this chapter, life is a box of surprises. And to our advantage, the gift of hurt teaches us what someone else's pain feels like. This is why God is so good in comforting the person who has lost a loved one through death. God Himself knows what it feels like. He lost His own Son. His Son was murdered in front of His mother! God knows what pain is and this is why He can be our hope in the most painful seasons of life. Hurt isn't always a negative.

All the hurts that I have experienced and still walking around with today only taught me to be sensitive to those who are in their first five minutes of pain. Someone who has not gone through mourning, hurt, and depression finds it difficult to understand the person who is in the season of hurt. If you know anything about grief, everyone mourns differently, but we all experience the same thing—hurt! I may not win every

**ALL THE HURTS THAT I HAVE EXPERIENCED AND STILL WALKING AROUND WITH TODAY ONLY TAUGHT ME TO BE SENSITIVE TO THOSE WHO ARE IN THEIR FIRST FIVE MINUTES OF PAIN.**

battle, but I have certainly acquired a lot of knowledge about myself with this unorthodox, disguised gift of hurt.

## HURT IS THE GREATEST TEACHER

Someone once said: "Mistakes are not only the greatest teacher. They are also the costliest." I will have to say that being hurt must come with a price. Someone can't learn how being hurt feels from someone else. You have to learn it by experiencing it for yourself. You can be prescribed a pain killer for an injury, but eventually, the pain killer will wear off. We must feel the pain to be able to minister to the *hurting*. I have learned that if I want to make an impact on someone's life, I need to ask myself three important questions about that person.

1. What makes people dream? (Their visions)
2. What makes people laugh? (Their joys)
3. What makes people cry? (Their hurts)

Just because we've read about "hurt" doesn't mean that we can automatically teach how to heal to others. Many people teach leadership lessons and material they haven't yet made their own. I remember when I enrolled for Bible School, I signed up in Biblical Studies. Normally, a pastor would first get his degree, then apply for a position as pastor of a church. As for me, I first got the position, then approximately seven years later or so, I enrolled for Bible School. Fortunately, I was given some school credits for something the

**JUST BECAUSE WE'VE READ ABOUT "HURT" DOESN'T MEAN THAT WE CAN AUTOMATICALLY TEACH HOW TO HEAL TO OTHERS.**

5

school called practicum. In other words, I had enrolled in some practiced studies in the field of the pastorate. I have been worked on and built up with pastoral skills.

**THE MORE HURT YOU HAVE SEEN OR EXPERIENCED, THE HIGHER YOUR CHANCES OF BEING A TEACHER OF IT.** Likewise, hurt is the greatest teacher. The more hurt you have seen or experienced, the higher your chances of being a teacher of it. I'm not saying you should go out and look for how you can get hurt here and there. I'm just saying that some of you, with the extent of hurt you have passed through in your lifetime, you would probably have a Masters, and for some, a Doctorate in the major I'll call HURT.

## HURT IS WHAT CHRIST ENDURED

The Governor and his wife knew that Jesus was an innocent man. Therefore, the Governor publicly washed his hands in a bowl of water and announced to the crowd that day that his hands would be cleaned of this man's innocent blood, and that it would fall on the people's hands for the decision of an innocent man's blood. The crowd's response that day was: "We will take responsibility for his death—we and our children!" Wow! That must have hurt in essence to hear people say; *we hate you so much we'll put the judgment of our deeds on ourselves and kids.* Then the governor turned Jesus over to them to be crucified. So, they took Jesus away.

Condemned prisoners had to carry their crosses to the execution site. Although His walk would be just under ½ of a mile, Jesus was so weakened from the beatings that He had taken from the Roman soldiers.

He was unable to carry His cross any further. We must remember that Jesus was carrying the crossbar (the patibulum) across His shoulders, and it weighs between 80 and 110 pounds, and it was also an uphill journey! He had also lost a lot of blood and fluids from His frequent beatings and bleeding. Isaiah prophesied that the messiah would hardly look human.

**Isaiah 52:14**

> "But many were amazed when they saw him. His face was so disfigured he seemed hardly human, and from his appearance, one would scarcely know he was a man."

If you can't call this hurt, you are not human. I understand that this was physical hurt, but it's still a hurtful experience. And Jesus Christ endured it for the sake of our salvation and His love towards us. As Jesus was dying for you and me at His execution site, the soldiers gave Jesus wine mixed with bitter gall, but when He had tasted it, He refused to drink it. He was offered this to help reduce His pain, but He refused to drink it. Gall is generally understood to be a narcotic that was used to deaden pain. Jesus would suffer fully conscious and with a clear mind.

As I imagined this event taking place as if I were in the crowd that day, I couldn't help but to recall the song called *When He was on the Cross (I was on His mind)*. A portion of the lyrics read:

**The look of love was on his face**
**Thrones were on his head**
**The blood was on his scarlet robe**
**Stained a crimson red**

7

Though his eyes were on the crowd that day
He looked ahead in time
For when he was on the cross
I was on his mind
For when he was on the cross
I was on his mind…

He *endured the cross* because of the joy that was set before Him, despising the shame, and is now set down at the right hand of the throne of God. He endured the cross of hurt. We must always remember that before there was a resurrection, there was first the Cross. There could be no resurrection without the Cross that preceded it. Every hurt we endure prepares us for the next one that approaches and makes us ready for the next person we encounter to help with their healing.

*To endure is to refuse to stray from your position in life.* Jesus could have called upon 12 legions of angels to deliver Him and destroy His enemies. Still, He held back from doing so because the Cross was the path that led us to our salvation and was His way of identifying and enduring with us in this thing called hurt.

## HURT IS NOT BEING WEAK BUT BEING STRONG

I know so many people who look down on someone who is hurt. Some people say things like "that person gets hurt too easy." I think that if we took the time to know why certain people get hurt easily, it's probably because in their past, they were hurt really bad! The fact of the matter is that they are still standing with a limp, and this speaks volumes of how strong they really are.

If you know anything about church life, yes, there are far greater good things in it than the opposite. The reason for the opposite is because "the church is built of 'PEOPLE' before it is built with 'PEWS.'" Somebody once said, "The **ONLY** thing that Jesus is coming back for are **PEOPLE**."

**There are two different areas a person needs healing from.**

1. *Hurt in the body* (Physical healing)
2. *Hurt by people* (Relational healing)

From a biblical perspective, you and I are not the only ones who have to deal with "Relational Healing." One of the strongest emotional and physical man in the Bible struggled with "Relational Healing"— **Paul the Apostle**. The Bible is gracious enough to give us some hope on how Paul dealt with "Relational Healing" in a letter that was written to Timothy near the last days of Paul's life.

> *"Get here as fast as you can. Demas, chasing fads, went off to Thessalonica and left me here. Crescens is in Galatia province, Titus in Dalmatia. Luke is the only one here with me. Bring Mark with you; he'll be my right-hand man since I'm sending Tychicus to Ephesus. Bring the winter coat I left in Troas with Carpus; also the books and parchment notebooks. Watch out for Alexander the coppersmith. Fiercely opposed to our Message, he caused no end of trouble. God will give him what he's got coming. At my preliminary hearing no one stood by me. They all ran like scared rabbits. But it doesn't matter—the Master stood by me and helped*

*me spread the Message loud and clear to those who had never heard it.
I was snatched from the jaws of the lion! God's looking after me…"*

—2 Timothy 4:9-18

## PAUL'S INSIGHT IN THIS LETTER GIVES US TRUTH TO THE REALITY OF RELATIONSHIPS

1. **You will have people who will disappoint you.**
   Demas, has deserted me (NAS)

2. **You will have people who will work against you.**
   *"Watch out for* Alexander the coppersmith. Fiercely opposed to our Message, *he caused* no end of trouble."

3. **Some relationships can be healed.**
   "Bring Mark with you; he'll be my right-hand man."

This was a beautiful ending for Paul the Apostle because earlier on in his ministry, the New Testament record indicates that a **"sharp contention"** developed between them. As far as the sacred record shows, these two remarkable men never saw one another again, up until this day when verse 11 mentions Paul's request for Timothy. This takes a strong man—to continue not just in the mission that he was assigned to in life but also to forgive and give second chances to someone who had been hurt previously in life.

"After a few days of this, Paul said to Barnabas,
'Let's go back and visit all our friends in each

of the towns where we preached the Word of God.
Let's see how they're doing.'
Barnabas wanted to take John along, the John nicknamed Mark.
But Paul wouldn't have him; he wasn't about to take along
a quitter who, as soon as the going got tough, had
jumped ship on them in Pamphylia. Tempers flared,
and they ended up going their separate ways: Barnabas
took Mark and sailed for Cyprus; Paul chose Silas."

—Acts 15:36-41

This statement is a testimony that people can grow up, people can change, relationships can be healed, and people can find working together again a positive experience.

Christ was not just hurt physically; He was also hurt relationally. Let's visit the Garden where we see clearly that Jesus is struggling in prayer. In my book, **dis.con.tinued**, I mention how man fell in the Garden of Eden, but Jesus redeems us in the Garden of Gethsemane. Jesus opened up and told His disciples His weaknesses: "My soul is crushed with grief to the point of death."

Mark writes, "Jesus became deeply troubled and distressed." And Luke writes: "He was in such agony of spirit that his sweat fell to the ground like great drops of blood."

Jesus just asked of one thing from His best friends—Peter, James, and John that day—"Keep watch and pray that you will not give in to temptation." Jesus prayed thrice that night, and each time He returned to check on Peter, James and John, He found them sleeping.

Jesus modeled how to respond versus how to react when it comes to being hurt. He didn't take their disobedience personal! Even though if there were any time He needed them to pray, it was that night.

> *"Then he came to the disciples and said,*
> *"Go ahead and sleep. Have your rest. But look—the time has come.*
> *The Son of Man is betrayed into the hands of sinners.*
> *Up, let's be going. Look, my betrayer is here!"*

> **—Matthew 26:45-46**

This cold-hearted evening, Judas arrives with a crowd of men armed with swords and clubs. Judas kisses Him, and Jesus says to him: ***"My friend, go ahead and do what you have come for."*** It's a picture of how Jesus' world was falling apart:

1. *He's in agony this night.*
2. *His best friends didn't pray for Him.*
3. *His disciple met Him with betrayal straight to His face after having another face the previous three and a half years. (This is what you call a two-faced at its finest).*
4. *Then Peter acts out in the flesh with attempted murder.*
5. *Jesus gets arrested.*

**BEFORE YOUR WORLD COMES TOGETHER, IT MUST FIRST FALL APART!**

"Before your world comes together, it must first fall apart!" Hurt doesn't make you weaker; it makes you better.

(Embracing my father Mondy Franco
just days before his passing.)

# CHAPTER TWO

# I'M SO MAD

*"Get mad, but not even, then get over it."*

—*Fernando E. Franco Sr.*

I'm so mad! I think all of us may have used this phrase at least once in our lifetime. At times, due to out carelessness, this phrase has gotten us into trouble or has caused some sort of offense on our journey in life.

I once heard a pastor share a bone-frightening illustration about a man who was bitten by a rabid dog. This was years before a treatment had been discovered for rabies. When it was determined that the dog was indeed rabid, the kind doctor told the man he had only a short time to live. Upon hearing this distressing news, the miserable man asked the doctor for some paper and a pencil and then set about writing intensely.

After a few minutes, the doctor interrupted, "If you are writing out your will, you still have time. Think carefully about your estate; you still have a few days."

The patient replied sharply, "Doc, I'm not making out my will. I am making a list of all the people I'm going to bite before I die!"

If someone hurts you, that doesn't make it right to hurt them back.

One of the quickest ways to fight back is with natural reflex. When we are put down, disrespected or OFFENDED, the natural reflex is to *REACT,* which then could produce *RAGE*. It's perfectly natural for most people to take offense when someone raises their voice at them or accuses them of something that's not their fault. I recall what the Book of Proverbs along with James in the Bible says:

**WHEN WE ARE PUT DOWN, DISRESPECTED OR OFFENDED, THE NATURAL REFLEX IS TO *REACT*, WHICH THEN COULD PRODUCE *RAGE*.**

**Proverbs 29:11**

> "A fool gives full vent to his anger, but a wise man keeps himself under control."

**James 1:19**

> "Post this at all the intersections, dear friends: Lead with your ears, follow up with your tongue, and let anger straggle along in the rear."

# LET IT GO

"Let It Go," the most popular song from Disney's 2013 animated musical, *Frozen*, was a smashing success. At the 86th Academy Awards, it won the award for Best Original Song.

Before we can examine the song, we must consider the events within the story which led up to "Let it go."

At the very beginning of the film, we learn that there are two sisters (princesses), who share a deep love for each other. However, everything goes wrong when Elsa, the older sister, accidentally freezes Anna's head (her younger sister) while using her magical powers to create an indoor winter wonderland. The princess's parents rush Anna off to be healed by some trolls.

Unfortunately, all memory of Elsa's powers must be swept from Anna's mind for her to be healed. So, Anna has no memory of what has occurred. After the event, Elsa is kept away from Anna so that she won't hurt her again, and in the years of separation that follow, a rift grows between them. Unfortunately, not too long, calamity strikes again, and the girls' parents are lost at sea.

When Elsa comes of age, the time for her coronation came. During the festivities, Anna falls in love with and is engaged to the impressive Prince Hans. Elsa, however, believes the two are acting too hastily, and won't allow it. In the ensuing fight, Elsa's powers are accidentally exposed. She then loses her composure and her ability to control her powers, resulting in a massive snowstorm and eternal winter that freezes the entire kingdom.

Having lost all self-control, hurting many people and their livelihoods, she storms into the mountains and starts singing "Let It Go" as she builds a castle of ice. The song begins by establishing the setting:

*"The snow glows white on the mountain tonight*
*Not a footprint to be seen*
*A kingdom of isolation,*
*And it looks like I'm the queen.*

She follows this by acknowledging her inner turmoil and her failure to control herself:

*"The wind is howling like this swirling storm inside*
*Couldn't keep it in, heaven knows I tried."*

Next, she sings about what she had previously been telling herself:

*"Don't let them in, don't let them see*
*Be the good girl you always have to be*
*Conceal, don't feel, don't let them know*
*Well, now they know."*

Somehow, the fact that the people now know about her power completely changes everything, and instead of trying to regain her composure, she decides to revel in her inner turmoil:

*"Let it go, let it go*
*Can't hold it back anymore*
*Let it go, let it go*
*Turn away and slam the door*

*I don't care*
*What they're going to say*
*Let the storm rage on,*
*The cold never bothered me anyway."*

I wonder how many of us can say that when we watched this film, Elsa was no longer Elsa? She had become us, the part of ourselves that we hate—the part that is mad, angry, and hurting the closest people to us because of it.

Elsa flaunted her powers, and she didn't care what people thought about them. The song continues...

*"My power flurries through the air into the ground*
*My soul is spiraling in frozen fractals all around*
*And one thought crystallizes like an icy blast*
*I'm never going back,*
*The past is in the past."*

As a child, Elsa and Anna are best friends and sisters, then Elsa almost kills Anna, after which the two are separated.

## "ANGER IS ONE LETTER SHORT OF DANGER"

**Although none of us are Disney characters, we can still have their nature.** When we as humans don't know how to take control of our anger and let it go, we can nearly kill someone. In some cases, loved ones have been killed because of it.

## THERE ARE FOUR CATEGORIES OF ANGER

1.  **Simmering Anger**
    This category of anger is usually stimulated by something that was done that could be considered unjust.

2.  **Burning Anger**
    This category is usually attached by a desire to avenge.

3.  **Fiery Anger**
    This category of anger is so fierce that it destroys common sense.

4.  **Blazing Anger**
    This category often results in loss of self-control, leading to extreme violence and possible temporal insanity.

## A SPITEFUL SON KILLS FOUR IN A FIT OF RAGE – JULY 8, 1928

To respect the family members, I'll change the names in this book. Rosanna, her son, and two hired workers were all shot dead on a secluded farm in Canada, while the rest of the family was away. Although nothing appeared to be stolen from the house and few clues were found, authorities determined that a rifle had caused the gunshot wounds. Not coincidentally, a rifle had been taken from a neighbor's farm just before the killings.

The investigation centered on the family—Rosanna's other son, Frank, in particular. Frank was known to have had problems with his mother, but he denied any involvement in the murders. After persistent interrogation failed to crack Frank, according to the article on History.com, a psychic who had reputedly solved crimes all over Europe by picking up "mind signals" from criminals, was summoned from Vienna, Austria. Using his alleged psychic powers, he sketched a scene that included a rifle hidden under some bushes. Using the sketch as a makeshift map, the police discovered the murder weapon near the family's personal home.

With this new evidence, Frank confessed to the crime! He had planned to kill his mother because he despised her with anger. The other three were killed only because they had stumbled on the scene. Frank expressed remorse only for killing his brother.

## MOSES KILLS WITH HIS ANGER – 1400'S B.C. (APPROXIMATELY)

Moses felt anger over the prejudiced treatment of his Hebrew brothers. But what he did with that anger is what caused all the trouble and eventually probably the greatest failure of his life.

**Moses allowed his anger to defeat him**. Acting on instinct, he committed a capital crime—he committed murder! Although Moses was right about the unfairness, he was wrong in his **RAGE**.

**WHAT HAD BEGUN AS SMOKE IN THE HEART OF MOSES, QUICKLY BURST INTO DEADLY FLAMES.**

What had begun as smoke in the heart of Moses, quickly burst into deadly flames. Perhaps no one noticed the angry sparks flying from his eyes, but his spirit was consumed with anger. The proof of it was in the crime.

Violence, in all of its various forms, has been a common characteristic of societies throughout human history. There are many theories about the causal factors associated with violence, but one in particular that is powerfully known is the General Strain Theory (GST) of crime.

According to GST, crime, including acts of violence, is the result of emotional strain in one's life. Strain can result from either losing something of value, such as a career *or* marriage, or it can result from failing to attain something of value, such as financial stability or educational goals. Strain can also result from having dysfunctional and strained personal relationships.

Strain in one's life leads to negative emotions such as *sadness*, *depression*, *anxiety*, or *anger*. According to GST, when negative emotions take the form of anger, they are most likely to lead to acts of crime, including violence.

This is not to say that anger resulting from strain always leads one to commit a crime. Obviously, that is not the case. We all get angry from time to time, but most of us do not respond to it by committing an act of crime. Some people yell and scream, while others may drink alcohol and get drunk. The stable ones simply wait a while and cool off.

# ANGER CAN KILL YOU IF YOU LET IT

**ANGER AND OTHER STRONG EMOTIONS CAN TRIGGER POTENTIALLY DEADLY HEART RHYTHMS IN CERTAIN VULNERABLE PEOPLE,** Anger and other strong emotions can trigger potentially deadly heart rhythms in certain vulnerable people, U.S. researchers say.

Previous studies have shown that earthquakes, war, or even the loss of a World Cup soccer match can increase rates of death from sudden cardiac arrest, in which the heart stops circulating blood.

"It's definitely been shown in all different ways that when you put a whole population under a stressor, sudden death will increase," said Dr. Rachel Lampert of Yale University in New Haven, Connecticut, whose study appears in the Journal of the American College of Cardiology.

The study looked at how this affects the electrical system of the heart.

The study further examines 62 patients with heart disease and implantable heart defibrillators or ICDs that can detect dangerous heart rhythms or arrhythmias and deliver an electrical shock to restore a normal heartbeat.

"These were people we know already had some vulnerability to arrhythmia," Lampert said in a telephone interview. Patients in the study took part in an exercise in which they recounted a recent angry episode while Lampert's team did a test called T-Wave Alternans that measures electrical instability in the heart.

The team specifically asked questions to get people to relive the angry episode. "We found in the lab setting that yes, anger did increase this electrical instability in these patients," she said.

Next, they followed patients for three years to see which patients later had a cardiac arrest and needed a shock from their implantable defibrillator.

The people who had the highest anger-induced electrical instability were ten times more likely than everyone else to have an arrhythmia in the follow-up.

At the end of the study, it suggests that anger can be deadly! It says yes, anger really does impact the heart's electrical system in precise ways that can lead to sudden death.

## WHY CAN'T WE JUST LAUGH?

Humor is the Joker in the hand of life. There is no better card to play in life than the Joker. Humor has a way of making even a poor hand a winner. We all have had our share of a poor hand dealt to us in life. I mentioned in my first book, *dis.con.tinued*, that I had to learn how to start laughing at myself because if I don't, others will. We are the only ones who can make our own choice to turn our madness into gladness.

**HUMOR HAS A WAY OF MAKING EVEN A POOR HAND A WINNER.**

The Book of Proverbs says, "All the days of the oppressed are wretched, but the cheerful heart has a continual feast." The Bible declares that those who laugh on the inside, party all the time!

Disappointments can launch new dreams for us, depending if we take the opportunity. The best sales professionals in America understand that the word "NO" spelled backward is "ON." The search for someone to blame will always be a successful find.

I don't want to watch the news; I want to make the news. If you don't like the news, go out and make some of your own. Those who have a why to live can bear almost anything. I want to encourage you right at this moment. Search for a why to laugh. Can't we just laugh about it? Let's not get used to worrying; let's get rid of it. Worry corrodes and corrupts the mind. Don't worry about it, laugh about it. I say this will all due respect to those who are suffering the most severe trials in life. But when things get a little better, take my challenge and laugh.

I want to prophesy a word over your life on this date that you are reading this sentence in this chapter of my book, *to.be.continued.* I use this scripture as a point of prophecy over your life:

**Job 8:21**

> "He will yet fill your mouth with laughter and your lips with shouts of joy."

**LIFE IS NOT ABOUT WAITING FOR THE STORMS TO PASS; IT IS ABOUT LEARNING HOW TO DANCE IN THE RAIN.**

Be led by your dreams, not pushed by your problems. The best way to cheer yourself up is to try and cheer somebody else up. Life is not about waiting for the storms to pass; it is about learning how to dance in the rain.

Most people in this life are as happy as they make up their minds to be. As you finish this chapter, say to yourself: "Self! I've got my mind made up, and my heart is fixed, and I'm laughing with Jesus all the way."

(Me and my siblings at my dad's funeral.)

# CHAPTER THREE

# DROPPED CALLS AND INTERFERENCES

*"Studies display that an individual who is interrupted takes 50 percent longer to accomplish his task and he or she makes up to 50 percent more errors."*

—*Fernando E. Franco Sr.*

A while back, my wife Veronica and I went to the movie theater to see the movie *Gravity*, starring Sandra Bullock and George Clooney.

The movie is about two people who were sent by NASA to do some work in space. While in space, everything is going perfectly fine until something horrible happens, and then it all goes awry.

The movie is filled with intensity as Sandra Bullock finds herself all alone stranded in space with no contact with earth or anyone else!

She experiences some kind of INTERFERENCE between her and "Houston" (Earth).

I believe that one of the reasons we could *stay stuck on pause* is because of interferences and dropped calls between you and God. Paul, in the Bible, told the Galatians:

**Galatians 5:7**

> "You were running a good race. Who cut in on you to keep you from obeying the truth?"

The "who" that Paul mentions can often be our own self. *"Studies display that an individual who is interrupted takes 5 percent longer to accomplish his task, and he or she makes up to 50 percent more errors."*

Let me help you discover what could be some of life's interruptions that we face on a daily schedule.

## SPAM EMAIL

If you are like me at all, I can't stand the unrequested emails from people or entities that I did not give permission to? Somehow, they received my information as a third party. This, in the email folders, is called spam. I hate spam, even the food called spam.

Most of the time, spam mail will automatically be sent to your junk folder. Many of us have allowed spam emails to take over our lives.

Spiritual spam emails are interferences in our lives. They are junks to our lives and a waste of time. Don't let spam be an interference.

**WHEN WE GET CAUGHT UP IN THE TORNADO OF JUNK, WE WON'T HAVE TIME FOR PURITY.** When we get caught up in the tornado of junk, we won't have time for purity. It's the purity that moves us out of pause.

## DROPPED CALLS

Have you ever been on an important phone call, and out of nowhere, the call just drops? Depending on how important the call was will determine your level of inconvenience. I live in Southern California, and it's usually on the 405 freeway at a certain spot, right before I am entering the city of Palm Springs on the 10 freeway, where my calls get dropped. I know now not to begin a phone call near those areas. Interferences that we are aware of are the indicators that we need to avoid. Dropped calls are interferences in our prayer lives with God. I can't express the importance of valuing the privilege we all have with the direct access that has been given to us with the New Covenant that Jesus gave.

One of the seven last words that Jesus spoke from the cross was, "It is finished."

**John 19:28-30**

> Jesus knew that his mission was now finished, and to fulfill Scripture he said, "I am thirsty." A jar of sour wine was sitting there, so they soaked a

sponge in it, put it on a hyssop branch, and held it up to his lips. When Jesus had tasted it, he said, **"It is finished!"** *Then he bowed his head and gave up his spirit.*

Until this time, a complicated system of sacrifices had atoned for sins. Only through the sacrifice of an animal as a substitute was the only way people can be forgiven and become clean before God. Jesus here became the final sacrifice for sin. The word, "It is finished," is the same as "paid in full." Jesus came to finish God's work of salvation to pay the FULL PENALTY for our sins. You no longer need a mediator (interference) between you and God. There are no 405 freeways between yours and God's communication system. Get rid of all dropped calls today.

## CRAZY DRIVERS

According to my wife, I would fall into the classification of being a crazy driver. She says I get a honk a day, and she is absolutely correct. I really get a honk a day!

Recently, my wife, Veronica and I were having lunch with a married couple in our church. Their teenage son was present with us that day. He begins to tell me a story that he said would make me laugh. He goes on with his story and utters:

> *My mom and I were at an intersection in Oxnard. Then there's a car taking their sweet old time making a right turn at the signal light. My mom is on the opposite direction of that car that is taking*

*their sweet old time. My mom was mad because she wanted to make her left turn but couldn't because of this car. Then my mom begins to honk her horn, shouting out loud in the car, 'Man! Some old people just need to learn how to drive around here. Dang!'*

*When my mom and I pulled up next to the car, it was you, pastor, driving that car!*

Crazy drivers can be an interference to you, releasing pause and slowing down your journey to the roadmap of success. Don't let

**DON'T LET PEOPLE GET IN YOUR WAY OR LANE**

people get in your way or lane and be the chasm to your success. This leads me to the next point I'd like you to discover.

## VISION KILLERS

Have you ever had someone that finishes the story for you while you are telling it? Have you ever had someone who tells you that your dream is too big or impossible? They may not say it with their mouth, but they will tell you with their body language.

**IF I COULD KICK THE PERSON IN THE BEHIND WHO IS RESPONSIBLE FOR MOST OF MY DREAMS NOT COMING TO PASS, I WOULDN'T BE ABLE TO SIT DOWN FOR TWO WEEKS.**

The people around us are not our biggest problem. We are our biggest problem. "If I could kick the person in the behind who is responsible for most of my dreams not coming to pass, I wouldn't be able to sit down for two weeks."

## Four vision killers and how you can stop them

### 1. Negativity

From others or even from yourself. When we listen to this malicious chatter, it prevents us from moving forward. It's suffocating. It's discouraging. It takes our focus off God and magnifies every weakness we have. We can't pursue our dreams when we're filled with negative words and toxic people reminding us "how it can't be done, why it shouldn't be done, and 101 reasons why you're not the person to do it." The negative mindset can take many forms, but they're all vision killers—cynicism, sarcasm, jealousy, bitterness, and silence.

*How To Stop Negativity?*

Choose to listen to God's voice over the voices of others. You have control over what you allow into your thoughts and mind and what you choose to believe.

### 2. Self-doubt

Quite possibly the biggest threat to your dream. Because if the enemy can get you to doubt yourself, he knows he's pretty much won. Doubt will leave every longing on the table, with a list of reasons why you're "not enough." You'll look at things from a million different angles, yet still come back to this one dangerous conclusion—**I can't do it.**

*How To Stop Self-doubt?*

Choose to believe what God says about you. He's the One who created you and put the vision in your heart! He whispers to you, "You have a purpose, you are valuable, you are amazing, and your life has meaning…"

## 3. Fear

Paralyzing, gripping, stop-you-dead-in-your-tracks kind of fear. Fear of people, fear of rejection, fear of failure, and fear of the unknown can take different forms, but they all lead to one result—PAUSE! You won't move forward.

*How To Stop Fear?*

Choose to trust God. Fear has won, until you determine in your heart that you will keep taking steps forward, no matter how small. Even with your knees knocking and your heart trembling, you stare it right in the face, believing more in the power of God over you than the fear that seeks to hold you back.

## 4. Procrastination

The lie—"You don't have time." But really, the truth may be that we don't want to *make time. It seems too difficult. It's going to cost us something. We're already weary from other life responsibilities, why add to the madness? Days slip by into months* and then into years. These are moments in time we can never get back. "It's too late for us anyway," we reason in our thoughts that still seek to urge us on. Or, *"I'll get to it when I really have* the time to focus on it." *Yet*, that day never comes because we mistakenly believe we have an endless supply of tomorrows.

### How To Stop Procrastination?

Choose to pray and move forward as God leads and opens new doors. The truth is, we will always make time for what is most important to us. Maybe something else will have to go for a season. Perhaps we can't keep doing everything we've always done, in order to focus on achieving our dream.

Don't let others steal your dream, giving them control to dash your hopes. It's too important to lay it down so carelessly.

**DON'T LET OTHERS STEAL YOUR DREAM, GIVING THEM CONTROL TO DASH YOUR HOPES.**

Don't allow fear, self-doubt, negativity, and procrastination to prevent you from going where He is leading you to go. God desires to do great things through you. He gives purpose and calling. We only have one chance at this life, make it count for His glory.

In going back to the movie, *Gravity*, when we lose connection, signal, or contact with the one who is ultimately in charge of us, our lives become endangered. The fact of the matter is that everywhere we go, whatever we do, someone or something will interfere with what we are doing, including ourselves.

God wants to have an intimate relationship with His creatures. He is a jealous God. For Adam & Eve, unfortunately, it did not take long.

This intimacy or union between God and man, between the Creator and His creatures, was interrupted over a piece of fruit.

- They disobeyed God.
- They pulled the plug that brought them to life.
- They separated themselves from the source of life.

Now, pain, suffering, and death had become their life.

## If…

If God is the source of life, then separation
from Him will naturally bring death.

If God is the source of happiness, then separation
from Him will only bring sadness.

If God is the source of love, then separation
from Him will bring hatred.

If God is the source of wisdom, then separation
from Him leads to foolishness.

If God is the source of order, then separation
from Him brings confusion.

If God is the source of blessing, then
separation from Him brings curses.

Usually, it's injuries, running out of breath and sometimes, even small bugs that interfere with our race.

# Do not…

**Do not** allow the cares of the world to suffocate us.

**Do not** allow our employers to dictate when we can worship God.

**Do not** allow the sufferings to shatter our hopes.

**Do not** allow the extensive waves of sin to
stifle the growth of your faith.

**Do not** allow the temporary joy that the world is offering for the
eternal joy that God is promising.

As this chapter ends, please continually keep on your mind that God uses the nameless, faceless, and useless. So, release the pause button and…

**GOD USES THE NAMELESS, FACELESS, AND USELESS.**

**Get Up
Look Up
Climb Up**

(Me at Lake Casitas in Ojai, California
for a time of separation with God.)

35

# CHAPTER FOUR

# KICK YOUR HEELS OFF AND RUN

*"It's not how tall we can stand but how low we can bow."*

—*Fernando E. Franco Sr.*

I remember being at a professional boxing event in Los Angeles, California. When the fight had ended, and 20,000 people exited the arena, a real fight broke out on the parking lot. My heart was pumping 100 miles an hour because my daughter was with me that day. Then we found ourselves caught in the middle of the entire fight happening just ten feet away from us. It was not my choice to be in the middle; neither was it my desire to put my daughter in harm's way. I had no choice. My car just so happened to be parked at the epicenter of where it all began.

The fight was interesting. It was seven grown men, approximately in their early twenties, against just one teenager. However, the teenager's

60-year-old father was in their car when he saw the fight begin. The father's instinct couldn't help but to step out of the car and assist his son in the fight. The seven young men could care less about how old the father was. They were in a zone—two against seven in the parking lot at the Staples' Center in Los Angeles, California. I must admit, this fight was so much better than the one that had just ended in the arena that day.

In the midst of the parking lot fight, out of nowhere, I witnessed this older woman running towards the scene and directly to the middle of this street fight! I couldn't believe my eyes. What I saw was that she had one of her high heels in her hand, and the other one was missing off her right foot. Then she starts swinging her high heel at all of the seven men that were fighting against her son and husband. Out of her mouth came a ton of explicit language as she shouted, "Leave my son alone you dirty filthy #*&!!"

## IT'S TIME TO RELEASE THE PAUSE BUTTON

There was a woman in the Bible with no name, just identified with a problem. She was sick of her life being on pause. She wanted to get back in the game. She was *dis.con.tinued* but wanted *to.be.continued*. She had been subjected to bleeding for twelve years and had suffered a great deal under the care of many doctors and had spent all she had. Yet, instead of getting better, she grew worse.

I'm almost positive that this woman wasn't wearing high heels, but if she were, when she heard Jesus was in town, she would have kicked her heels off and started running! Run where?

Not away, not to an addiction, but into the arms of Jesus!

**SHE PRESSED IN, PRESSED ON, AND PRESSED PLAY. SHE WAS IMPETUOUS.** Her life was on pause for 12 years, and she wasn't going to let another year go by. This day in the Bible, she pressed in, pressed on, and pressed play. She was impetuous.

Impetuous people don't care what anyone thinks or says. They will go where no one else would and will not allow anything to stop them. They will do desperate things because that's who they are—impetuous people.

## KICK YOUR HEELS OFF AND GET RUNNING

Ladies? Heels may make you "look" good, but you can't "fight" good nor "run" good in them. Yes, you will stand taller in them, but God is not looking for height; He's looking for humility. It's not how tall we can stand but how low we can bow.

**SOMETIMES, WE HAVE TO GET RID OF THE WASTE BEFORE YOU CAN TASTE.** This woman bowed low enough to get Jesus to stop what He was doing and get her *to.be. continued*, up and going. Emptiness is the prerequisite for desperation. Sometimes, we have to get rid of the waste before you can taste.

Desperate can be defined in three different ways:

1. Dangerously reckless or violent as from urgency or despair.
2. Showing extreme courage, especially of actions courageously undertaken as a last resort.

38

3.  Showing utmost urgency or intensity, mainly because of great need or desire.

Allow me to translate it this way. Blessed are the desperate, for they will tear the roof off if and when necessary. Blessed are the desperate, for if it were not for them, the presence and the power of God would rarely be manifested in the church.

It's not religion, ceremony, tradition, methods, or programs that will get you from *dis.con.tinued—to.be.continued.* It's true and tested desperation that will launch you off the runway and flying high in the sky.

## 10 WAYS TO BE DESPERATE

**Desperate** beyond comfort
**Desperate** beyond reputation
**Desperate** beyond tradition
**Desperate** beyond cosmetics
**Desperate** beyond emotions
**Desperate** beyond reason
**Desperate** beyond others
**Desperate** beyond measures
**Desperate** enough to risk ridicule
**Desperate** enough to risk failure.

When you become desperate, people will criticize you and look at you as **overboard, extreme, unusual,** and weird.

**WHEN YOU BECOME DESPERATE, PEOPLE WILL CRITICIZE YOU AND LOOK AT YOU AS OVERBOARD, EXTREME, UNUSUAL, AND WEIRD.**

People will try to hold you down and shut you up. Just like the woman in the Bible, you may get your fingers stepped on, and possibly your feelings crushed. But the bottom line is this; if you truly become desperate, then you will get what you are asking for.

## DON'T WAIT AROUND FOR GOD TO TOUCH YOU

This woman was positive in her mind that Jesus wasn't going to touch her. Her mindset very well could have been because of the Levitical law that was in place concerning this matter.

**Leviticus 15:19**

> "When a woman has her regular flow of blood, the impurity of her monthly period will last seven days, and anyone who touches her will be unclean till evening."

After twelve years with this condition and with the law set in her timeline, there was no way a person was going to touch her! For a person to touch her, according to the Law, would mean that they themselves would now be declared unclean. This is why she only touched Jesus' clothes and not His body.

This poor woman hadn't felt the warmth from another human beings' hand or touch in a long time. I can't imagine the position of loneliness she had to settle for in life. However, she was not going to take it one minute longer. Enough was enough. She was not going to wait around for God to touch her. She was going to touch Him!

## IT BEGINS WITH JUST A THOUGHT

When she heard about Jesus, she came up behind Him in the crowd and touched His cloak, because she *thought*, "If I just touch his clothes, I will be healed."

While in Bible School (Christian Psychology class), I was taught something called "Self-Talk." Sometimes, you got to talk to yourself, as long as it is not WITH yourself. So, go ahead, talk yourself into pressing the play button. Let's get up; let's get going, and let's get continued.

**I WAS TAUGHT SOMETHING CALLED "SELF-TALK." SOMETIMES, YOU GOT TO TALK TO YOURSELF, AS LONG AS IT IS NOT WITH YOURSELF.**

There's a story about an elderly man who was on his death bed ready to die. He called over his wife to his side and said, "Honey, when I die, I want to be cremated." She asked, "Why do you want to be cremated and NOT PLACED IN A COFFIN?"

He answered, "Honey, I've been restricted to a BOX for the entire 92 years of my life; I don't want to be buried in one."

If people don't understand you, that's okay. If some get upset because you don't fit into their world, don't worry about it. If they want to stay in the same condition for another twelve years, all we can do is lead by example. Some people may try and bury your dream, but they don't realize that your dream is a seed. They'll see you walk on water and say it's because you can't swim. Just keep leading by example. Everyone will always have their opinion about you, but what do you say about yourself? What are your thoughts about you?

If you try to keep everyone happy, the one person that will never be happy is you. I've learned the hard way. Your time is too valuable to worry about pleasing everyone else or making them happy.

Don't you think this woman with the issue of blood could have come up with 101 excuses why she wouldn't be able to touch Jesus?

- She was too weak from the loss of blood.
- She was tired of trusting men.
- She was overtopped by the crowd around her.
- She was up against legality issues.

But it began with just a thought, "If I could only touch Jesus, what would life be like?"

**AT TWENTY YEARS OLD, WE WONDER WHAT EVERYBODY THINKS ABOUT US, AND AT FORTY YEARS OLD, WE DON'T CARE WHAT ANYBODY THINKS ABOUT US. THEN AT SIXTY YEARS OLD, WE REALIZE NOBODY WAS EVEN THINKING ABOUT US.**

Somebody once said, "At twenty years old, we wonder what everybody thinks about us, and at forty years old, we don't care what anybody thinks about us. Then at sixty years old, we realize nobody was even thinking about us."

## EXCHANGE WHAT YOU GOT FOR WHAT HE HAS

The word, "touch," in the story concerning the woman with the blood condition, is the Greek word, *HAPTOMAI*, which means "to attach oneself to."

Once you touch Him, don't let go! Attach yourself. Our problem is that we let go right before Jesus was about to look our way. This woman came across one heck of a deal this day. She exchanged what she had for what Jesus owned. She had a sickness; Jesus had healing. She had loneliness; Jesus had warmth. She had nothing, but Jesus had everything.

The pause button on life was immediately released, and the play button was going. This time, twelve years later, the song sounded a lot better than it was playing the first time.

She exchanged her weakness for His power—the very same power that the Founder of creation used to create man out of the dust of the ground. The same power God used to stretch a measuring line across the boundary oceans. What a deal! This was a no-brainer. Your turn!

**Ephesians 3:20**

> "Now to him who is able to do immeasurably more than all we ask or imagine, according to his power that is at work within us..."

## 10 WAYS THAT GOD IS IMMEASURABLY MORE THAN ENOUGH

### When you are in pain

2 Corinthians 1:3-4: "Blessed be the God and Father of our Lord Jesus Christ, the Father of mercies and God of all comfort, who

comforts us in all our affliction, so that we may be able to comfort those who are in any affliction, with the comfort with which we ourselves are comforted by God."

## When you are confused

Philippians 4:7: "And the peace of God, which surpasses all understanding, will guard your hearts and your minds in Christ Jesus."

## When you are scared

Deuteronomy 31:6: "Be strong and courageous. Do not fear or be in dread of them, for it is the LORD your God who goes with you. He will not leave you or forsake you."

## When you are broken

Psalms 147:3: "He heals the brokenhearted and binds up their wounds."

## When you are stressed

1 Peter 5:7: "Give all your worries and cares to God, for he cares about you."

## When you are weak

Isaiah 40:29: "He gives strength to the weary and increases the power of the weak."

## When you are hungry

Philippians 4:19: "And my God will supply every need of yours according to his riches in glory in Christ Jesus."

## When you are tired

Matthew 11:28: "Come to me, all who labor and are heavy laden, and I will give you rest."

## When you are lonely

2 Corinthians 6:18: "And I will be a father to you, and you shall be sons and daughters to me, says the Lord Almighty."

## When you are abused

Thessalonians 3:3: "But the Lord is faithful. He will establish you and guard you against the evil one."

Kick your heels off and run. Run as fast as you can or at a reasonable pace. If it has to begin with a crawl, do so. Also, if it has to start with a walk, walk and then run. So be it! But what you don't want to do is to stay stuck on pause for too long.

(View of the Staples Center at night *Photo Tripadvisor.com*)

## CHAPTER FIVE

# THE OX OF OXNARD

*"No matter how hard you work, there is probably someone else in your city that is always working harder."*

—*Fernando E. Franco Sr.*

I wake up every day Monday-Saturday no later than 4:00 A.M. My usual time is 3:30 A.M., but no later than 4:00 A.M. I don't use an alarm clock, I don't set my I-phone to alert me, nobody wakes me up other than *passion*. I love waking up super early because there's no distractions. No emails to return, no phone calls to answer, no texts to return. Don't misinterpret me, I'm not saying that there is none of the above to do, neither am I saying that I don't like to return emails, calls, etc. I'm saying that 3:30-4:00 A.M is too early to do any of what I listed above. Nobody will answer, check their emails, you get the picture.

At so early in the morning, I'm able to meditate, pray and have my devotional time with God. I'm able to feed myself for the purpose of my own personal nourishment. As a pastor, I'm constantly preparing meals for the congregation, podcasts, and others.

**IT'S PASSION THAT WAKES ME UP.** As I mentioned, there is one thing that wakes me up this early every day besides the grace of God. PASSION! It's passion that wakes me up.

Months before I began to write my first book *dis.con.tinued*, whenever I went to sleep, I prayed to God not to wake me up. Depression and loneliness had such their tight grip on me I didn't want to live, let alone wake up to face the oppressive giant of that day. Today, I can't believe the passion that has returned to me. But it didn't just return on its own, I sought it, hungered for it and reconditioned it. Now, it's back alive and well!

I find myself writing this chapter at exactly 2:04 A.M because of passion. I went to sleep last night at 9:00 P.M. and the passion I have writing this book woke me up at 1:00 A.M. to read, and have mediation with God. I couldn't wait to write this chapter that has burning deep with fire in me to give to you, the reader of this book.

I have found that there's a unique pattern that the successful ones of today, yesterday and tomorrow all have in common. Successful people are not just those who make a lot of money, they are simply impactful. They come up with solutions for problems, medications for illnesses, strategies for long term results and global change. The successful giants have this one unique habit in common. They make more time than the average people.

**THE SUCCESSFUL GIANTS HAVE THIS ONE UNIQUE HABIT IN COMMON. THEY MAKE MORE TIME THAN THE AVERAGE PEOPLE.**

**The successful** – Make more time.
**The mediocre** – Don't use their time.
**The lazy** – Allow time to vanish.

## SUCCESSFUL PEOPLE MAKE MORE TIME

*Successful people* make more time. We all have the same amount of time. Not one of us have more time than others. I don't care if you are a celebrity, millionaire, or professional. We all have the same amount of time. Twenty-four hours every day. However, the difference is what the successful DO with their time. Giants of success MAKE MORE TIME.

**GIANTS OF SUCCESS MAKE MORE TIME.**

For example, let's take a look at a professional sports athlete like Kobe Bryant, Michael Jordan, Tiger Woods, Julio Caesar Chavez and Fernando Vargas. They all have one thing in common. While everyone else is sleeping, they are practicing, training, running, and working hard on what they want to become – the greatest of all time. They have become the best ever because they made more time. They were up at 3:00A.M. while their challengers were waking up at 10:00 A.M.

The professional boxer that is running 10-15 miles every day at 4:00A.M. wants to be a champion. The average boxer wonders why he loses his wind in the 11th round and can't contend with the champion. It's because in the world of professional boxing the 11th and 12th rounds are what are called the championship rounds and very few can fight those rounds. The ones who make more time and train for it can.

## MEDICORE PEOPLE DON'T USE THIER TIME

*The mediocre* have way more potential than they realize. They believe in everyone else except themselves. They will work hard for someone above them but will not work hard for their own life. They have bought into someone else's vision but never acquired one of their own.

They are great followers but horrible leaders. What is a horrible leader you may ask? A horrible leader is not one who just treats others bad, a horrible leader is one who can't lead himself.

Mediocre people will use time, but not their own. They use other people's time. They are working for someone else eight hours a day,

**MEDIOCRE PEOPLE WILL USE TIME, BUT NOT THEIR OWN. THEY USE OTHER PEOPLE'S TIME.**

but when they get home they don't work on something that could make them successful. Don't get me wrong. You may be working for a company that is making a significant impact but what if God wants you to do the same or possibly something even bigger and better than the company you are currently working for? You'll never know! If you are only operating on someone else's time, you'll live with a would if question mark when you turn 80 years old. Mediocre people don't use their time. They use someone else's.

## LAZY PEOPLE ALLOW TIME TO VANISH

**THE LAZY DON'T KNOW THEY EVEN HAVE TIME! THEY DON'T KNOW THAT TIME IS SLIPPING AWAY.**

*The lazy* don't know they even have time! They don't know that time is slipping away. They have no idea that one day they woke up at their 50<sup>th</sup> birthday party and fell into a state of severe depression because they thought their life amounted to nothing. Vanished, gone, disappeared. Nothing to show for.

Don't get discouraged if this is your category in life at the moment. This book is designed to move you from *dis.con.tinued-to.be.continued.* Let me help you. Keep reading and your life will change. You still got at least another good solid 30 years on you to put into life and see a harvest return that will put a smile on your face and a peace in your heart.

God loves all the three the same, there's no favoritism with the successful over those who don't use their time or allow time to pass them by. However, what the successful get out of life is going to be different. It's the law of sowing and reaping. What you put in this life is what you'll get out of it.

Whenever you look at the successful and say I wish I had what they have. Ask yourself, can I do what they do? Success just didn't fall into their lap by accident. They worked for it. Oh, I'm sorry. I didn't mean to cuss in this book, but I did say the word work. They didn't just work for it, but they worked extraordinarily hard and continue to work hard because they want to be the greatest at what they do. This is called being good stewards of what God has gifted you to do on this planet.

**WHENEVER YOU LOOK AT THE SUCCESSFUL AND SAY I WISH I HAD WHAT THEY HAVE. ASK YOURSELF, CAN I DO WHAT THEY DO?**

Most lottery winners who become multi-millionaires overnight usually lose what they inherited or won in a certain matter of time. It's interesting to find that those who inherit something that is valuable will eventually lose it or have to hand it over to someone who can keep it alive to start reproducing. Parents know, if you buy your child their car, versus if they bought their own car. It usually works out that the child will take better care of their car when they are the ones who bought it and are making the monthly payments on it.

## THE OX OF OXNARD

I was born, raised and still reside in the city of Oxnard, California. Many great professional athletes, actors and large cooperation's are based out of Oxnard, California. My city is also known for its agriculture.

**Proverbs 14:4**

> *"Where there are no oxen, the manger is empty,*
> *but from the strength of an ox come abundant*
> *harvests."*

Where no oxen are, the barn is clean, but increase is by the strength of the ox. What we see in this verse is a tension between the desire for a *"clean"* barn and the need for a *"filled"* barn.

The growth of a church or any living organism will always require TENSION.

Church growth is not cheap, church growth is not free, you can't even INHERIT church growth. There is ALWAYS a price to pay for GROWTH.

Proverbs 14 sends us a message that If you want a sweet-smelling, picture perfect, little show-place of a barn, you'd better not put any oxen in there! On the other hand, if you want a **full barn**, you'll need to get some oxen.

And whenever you're dealing with oxen (people) you're going to have to put up with the mess they're going to make.

Clean barns are nice looking. But if you think about it, the purpose of a barn is *not* to be **CLEAN**, but to be **FILLED**. The great news for my church is that we got a big mess!!! The mess simply means that we are GROWING!!!!

## THE OX IN THE BIBLE

Where I live and reside has always been an agricultural city. At one time Oxnard, California was the strawberry capital of world. I remember one day Veronica and I being in Times Square, New York City and purchasing a small container of strawberries. Flipping the container upside down I find the label that read "grown in Oxnard, California." I literally live across the street from one of the biggest strawberry fields in Oxnard. I have seen quite a bit of agriculture in the 49 years of my life. Tractors, water, plowing, dirt, you get the picture.

In the bible, the ox was the farmer's tractor. He plowed with it. He watered his crops with it. He harvested with it. He ground his flour with it. The more oxen, the more productivity!

On the other hand, the ox was also a source of trouble to the farmer. The ox had to be fed daily, and it took a lot of feed to satisfy the appetite of the working ox. The ox had to be sheltered from the wet and cold in order to stay healthy. Oxen had to be penned in, so they didn't wander off and get into trouble. They had to be doctored when sick or injured, and oh, what a smelly mess that would be found in the barn.

Do you see the tension here? Dealing with an ox is worth all the trouble if you care about filling the barn. But if what you care about is a clean barn, then by all means, get rid of the ox.

*"David Livingstone went to the darkest parts of Africa as a lone missionary. After some time, his missions committee wrote to him saying,*

*"Some people would like to join you. What's the easiest road to get where you are?" He replied, "If they're looking for the easiest road, tell them to stay in England. I want people who will come, even if there's no road at all!"*

The reality is that great vision, great hearts, great skill, and great gifts aren't quite enough for success to come to past. It takes an unstoppable spirit and hard work to make great things happen. Working with God, on yourself and with people.

**THE UNSTOPPABLE SPIRIT IN A PERSON IS WHAT MAKES AN UNSTOPPABLE CHURCH IN A CITY AND AN UNSTOPPABLE BUSINESS IN A NATION.**

The unstoppable spirit in a person is what makes an unstoppable church in a city and an unstoppable business in a nation.

## UNSTOPPABLE PEOPLE ARE

Unbeatable
Relentless
Unrestrainable
Unyielding
Never quitting
A giving selection of people in a crowd
Have the gift of endurance
They cannot be kept from moving forward
They are not discouraged by anything they hear
They will not be limited to the point of restraint
They have supernatural forward movement in their spirit

## HAVE YOU MET THIS UNSTOPPABLE MAN?

He was beaten, he was stoned, he was publicly criticized, he was jailed, he was forsaken by his ministry companions. But he **con.tin. ued** to build the church. Ladies and gentlemen meet Paul the apostle. Paul was handed in life the worst situations and made it the best situation!

He was put in jail, BUT HE WITNESSED TO THE JAILERS. He was forgotten about in jail, BUT HE WROTE LETTERS FROM JAIL to strengthen the congregations. He was thrown in jail, BUT HE CONTINUED TO DISCIPLE YOUNG TIMOTHY from jail. He was doing time in jail, BUT HE DID NOT PAUSE WHY? – He was UNSTOPPABLE!

*"We often miss opportunity because it's dressed*
*in overalls and looks like work"*

—Thomas A. Edison

## SUCCESSFUL MIRACLES IN THE BIBLE WERE SOLELY NOT SPIRITUAL BUT PHYSICAL

One of the most famous miracles in the bible is when Jesus turned water into wine. Often, people will quote the miracle with leaving out all the physical work it still required.

## JOHN 2:1-6

*"On the third day a wedding took place at Cana in Galilee. Jesus' mother was there, and Jesus and his disciples had also been invited to the wedding. When the wine was gone, Jesus' mother said to him, "They have no more wine." "Woman, why do you involve me?" Jesus replied. "My hour has not yet come." His mother said to the servants, "Do whatever he tells you."* **Nearby stood six stone water jars, the kind used by the Jews for ceremonial washing, each holding from twenty to thirty gallons."**

Water weighs about 8.33 lbs. per gallon. That means each stone jar held 167-250 lbs. of water Which also means that some PHYSICAL WORK was involved in carrying these big bad boys.

In Israel the banquet rooms were all held upstairs. Climbing stairs would have been involved in this successful miracle.

The water systems in these days (ancient cities) all came from a central source. Which would have meant there was a journey involved in this process of filling up these jars.

Jesus set up this miracle so that people had to do some physical work that didn't involve nothing spiritual or mystical. The practical application is most of the time success looks like a lot of work.

Jesus went on to tell them *"Fill them to the brim!"* Jesus said to the servants, "Fill the jars with water"; so, they filled them to the brim. Then he told them, **"Now draw some out and take it to the master of the banquet."**

The master of the banquet tasted the water that had been turned into wine. He did not realize where it had come from, but the **servants** who had drawn the water knew. Notice, the word servants. When the servants work, the miracle/success proceeds.

**Proverbs 18:9**

> *"Whoever is lazy regarding his work is also a brother to the master of destruction."*

If you've been stuck on pause in lazy workmanship, the best response to this is to simply repent, turn away and commence to do the hard work of leadership. The benefits will be extraordinary!

*"Successful people are not gifted; they just work hard, then succeed on purpose."*

—G.K. Nelson

(Oxnard California *Photo Realtor.com*)

(Me, at *16 yrs old* in front of the house
I grew up in Oxnard, California.)

(With Oxnard's 3X Boxing's World Champion Fernando Vargas)

# CHAPTER SIX

# LACE UP YOUR BOOTS AND THROW SOME PUNCHES

*"Soldiers fight not because they hate what is in front
of them, but because they love what is behind them."*

—*Fernando E. Franco Sr.*

In chapter three, I addressed mainly the women about kicking their heels off and running. If I can encourage men with any chapter, it would have been this one—lace up your boots and throw some punches!! Let's consider a scripture about this truth:

*When Gideon came to the Jordan, he and the three hundred men who were with him crossed over, **exhausted but still in pursuit**.*

The tenacity to fight and keep fighting is the key element that separates the genius from the ordinary!

**THE TENACITY TO FIGHT AND KEEP FIGHTING IS THE KEY ELEMENT THAT SEPARATES THE GENIUS FROM THE ORDINARY!**

It was Gideon's family whom he loved so much that gave him the reason to soldier up. It was what was behind him (family, his people) that he loved that gave him the tenacity to fight. Who are you fighting for? Think of their names. Picture your children's faces, your uncles and aunts, your spouse, and even your future spouse.

Gideon had torn down the altars of Baal (Satan). The Midianites and Amalekites were very angry with him. So angry that they wanted to kill him. But God placed His hand upon Gideon and protected him. Then God's call came to Gideon. Gideon didn't feel worthy of being used by the Lord. And he said to God, "**Oh my Lord, How can I save Israel? My family is poor in Manasseh, and I am the least in my father's house.**"

Gideon had **32,000 men** that were ready to go to war against the Midianites. But God said that was too many. (God didn't want Israel to brag about their accomplishments. He wanted to be the One to receive praise).

Every time Israel went into battle, the outcome was determined by one thing. It was not whether they were armed heavily enough, had a huge army, or knew proper military strategy. Every time Israel went into battle with obedience to God, they won. Every time they were disobedient, they lost.

I am surrounded by military bases where I live. During the past 30 years, many soldiers have been members of our church throughout their stay on bases nearby, and they have made our church their home church while being stationed here in Ventura County, California.

I have gotten to build many short terms and long term relationships with them as their pastor. In doing so, I have learned a little about armies.

## FIVE ACTUALITIES ABOUT ARMIES

### 1. ARMIES HAVE LEADERS

All armies have leaders, and God gives armies to a church, family, organization, and a company for a reason—"TO LEAD."

### 2. ARMIES HAVE ENEMIES

The enemy of the church and the child of God is Satan and his evil spirits. Our enemy is both "a roaring lion" and "an angel of light." He is both cruel and crafty.

### 3. ARMIES HAVE BANNERS

Every country has flags with the country's logo on them. The country's flag is the quintessential form of national brand and identity.

As long as we keep Jesus Christ as our banner and not a church logo as the banner, we will always remain a winning army.

### 4. ARMIES HAVE SOLDIERS

An army is made up of foot soldiers. Just like the women who kicked off their heels and ran, men need to lace up their boots and throw some punches.

One of God's greatest New Testament soldiers was Paul. One day, he invited Timothy, not to a potluck in the ministry, but a fight:

**2 Timothy 2:3-4**

> *"Join with me in suffering, like a good soldier of Christ Jesus. No one serving as a soldier gets entangled in civilian affairs, but rather tries to please his commanding officer."*

Soldiers are exactly that—"SOLDIERS!" They understand that they went through boot camp for a reason—to face a war!

**SOLDIERS CAN TAKE A PUNCH, THROW A PUNCH, AND AT TIMES, FIGHT WOUNDED.**

Soldiers can take a punch, throw a punch, and at times, fight wounded.

Every thinking person wishes that ARMIES were not necessary (just ask the mother of an 18-yr-old child killed in Afghanistan). However, just as there are enemies that would attack other nations, so the members of the church must be engaged against forces that would attempt to destroy them. In a war, the objective of the battle is NOT to kill enemy soldiers. The aim is to WOUND enemy soldiers.

When a soldier dies, in principle, his army has completed its duty to him. However, when a soldier is wounded, it takes an average of three other soldiers to care for him.

Satan knows that if he cannot kill those who belong to THE CHURCH. Then, his tactic would be to WOUND THE PEOPLE who belong to the church.

## 5. ARMIES HAVE ARMOR

Knowing that we have been given an armor for power and not using it will not accomplish anything, we must, therefore, exercise and use our God-given authority.

*I read a story about a man who was found dead in a small, shabby room that he rented for $3 a week. He had been a familiar sight on the streets of Chicago for about twenty years, always dressed in rags and eating out of the garbage cans.*

*One day, neighbors became concerned because they had not seen him for two to three days, and they later found him dead in bed. An autopsy revealed that he had died of malnutrition, yet a money belt found around his waist contained $23,000.00.*

*This man lived in poverty, peddling newspapers for a living, yet he had money. He could have lived in the finest hotel in town; instead, he lived in a little rundown room. He could have eaten the finest of foods instead of the garbage he chose for meals. But he did not use what belonged to him.*

We need to know what belongs to us. We need to know that we have AUTHORITY OVER demonic forces.

Lace up your boots! I mentioned that an army is made up of *foot* soldiers. Boots are designed to be worn on your feet. However, boots that are not worn are merely decoration or a showcase in a man's closet.

**BOOTS ARE DESIGNED TO BE WORN ON YOUR FEET. HOWEVER, BOOTS THAT ARE NOT WORN ARE MERELY DECORATION OR A SHOWCASE IN A MAN'S CLOSET.**

When Paul was describing the soldier's gear to the Ephesians, he explained part of the gear that deals with the Christian warriors' feet.

The boots (shoes) of the Roman soldiers were thick, reinforced, and had a nail-studded sole. The metal nail gave the warrior greater stability and quickness of movement. Their boots covered from the middle of the leg down with wide stripes of leather that securely fixed the shoes to the soles of their feet.

They were fitted securely to facilitate the rapid, non-slip foot movement necessary for hand-to-hand combat. Soldiers do not just lace up but throw punches. The ability to stand firm without slipping or falling was always the great help in battle. The soldier who lost his footing could lose his life!

The Christian, with his feet firmly planted in the Gospel of peace, will have confidence and assurance when he confronts his enemy. To attempt to stand against the enemy on any other ground than the Gospel of Jesus Christ as its footing is sure to cause defeat in that man's life.

It's the lacing up of our boots that brings the peace of God to keep us rooted in the rocky places of our battlefield. A soldier who cannot maintain his footing is useless in battle.

## WHEN GOD RECRUITS AN ARMY, HE IS LOOKING FOR:

### BRAVE PEOPLE

Judges 7:3

> Now announce to the army, 'Anyone who trembles with fear may turn back and leave Mount Gilead.' So twenty-two thousand men left, while ten thousand remained.

To map out a course of action and follow it to the end requires a brave man with enough bravery that only a soldier possesses.

*There's a story about a man who bragged that he had cut off the tail of a man-eating lion with only his pocket knife. When he was asked why he hadn't cut off the lion's head, the man replied: "Someone else had already done that."*

### SELFLESS PEOPLE

Judges 7:4-6

> But the Lord said to Gideon, "There are still too many men. Take them down to the water, and I will

*thin them out for you there. If I say, 'This one shall go with you,' he shall go; but if I say, 'This one shall not go with you,' he shall not go."*

*So Gideon took the men down to the water. There the Lord told him, "Separate those who lap the water with their tongues as a dog laps from those who kneel down to drink." Three hundred of them drank from cupped hands, lapping like dogs. All the rest got down on their knees to drink.*

Nine thousand and seven hundred men were only concerned with their thirst. They paid no attention to their fellow soldier or the enemy. We need to place God first by fulfilling the pledge we made to the Lord—to war!

## DEDICATED PEOPLE

**Judges 7:7**

*The Lord said to Gideon, "With the three hundred men that lapped I will save you and give the Midianites into your hands. Let all the others go home."*

From 32,000 men to just 300 men, this is huge! The army didn't want God as their recruiter. But God has never lost a battle with His selection.

I remember the first time I heard the worship song, "Never Lost" by Elevation and its writers (Songwriters: Christopher Joel Brown / Steven Furtick / Tiffany Hammer), I was lured in by its lyrics. The melody was incredibly catchy but there was something about the lyrics of "Never Lost."

### Never Lost
### <u>Elevation Worship</u>

"Miracles when You move
Such an easy thing for You to do
Your hand is moving right now
You are still showing up
At the tomb of every Lazarus
Your voice is calling me out
Right now, I know You're able
And my God, come through again

**You can do all things
You can do all things but fail
'Cause You've never lost a battle
No, You've never lost a battle
And I know, I know
You never will**

Everything's possible
By the power of the Holy Ghost
A new wind is blowing right now
Breaking my heart of stone
Taking over like it's Jericho

And my walls are all crashing down
But right now, I know You're able
And my God, come through again

**You can do all things**
**You can do all things but fail**
**'Cause You've never lost a battle**
**No, You've never lost a battle**
**And I know, I know**
**You never will**

You've never lost a battle (You've never lost a battle)
You've never lost a battle (You've never lost a battle)
You've never lost a battle (You've never lost a battle)
You never will (Oh, You never will)
You've never lost a battle (You've never lost a battle)
You've never lost a battle (You've never lost a battle)
You've never lost a battle (You've never lost a battle)
Never, never (You've never lost a battle)
So faithful
I know, I know, it's who You are

**You can do all (You can do all things)**
**You can do all things,**
**all things but fail (You can do all things but fail)**
**'Cause You've never lost a battle**
**No, You've never lost a battle**

Keep your boots laced up, throw punches, and stay in the army of Lord. And as long as God is your commander-in-chief, I've never seen Him lose a battle.

**AND AS LONG AS GOD IS YOUR COMMANDER-IN-CHIEF, I'VE NEVER SEEN HIM LOSE A BATTLE.**

*In his book,* One Crowded Hour, *Tim Bowden describes an incident in Borneo in 1964. Nepalese fighters known as Gurkhas were asked if they would be willing to jump from airplanes into combat against the Indonesians.*

*The Gurkhas didn't clearly understand what was involved, but they bravely said they would do it, asking only that the plane fly slowly over a swampy area and no higher than 100 feet. When they were told that the parachutes would not have time to open at that height, the Gurkhas replied, "Oh, you didn't mention parachutes before!"*

When God recruits an army, He is looking for dedicated people.

In our relationship with God, He calls us to be a part of His army. He is looking for the **brave**, **selfless**, and **dedicated** men who will lace up their boots and throw punches. Will you be one of them?

I surrendered my life to God in the early 1980s. I was raised singing a song during praise and worship that was called, "I'm Going to Stay on the Battlefield."

> I'm going to stay on the battlefield.
> I'm going to stay on the battlefield.
> I'm going to stay on the battlefield until I die!

I'm going to stay on the battlefield; I'm going to stay on the battlefield.
I'm going to stay on the battlefield until I die.

I'm going to watch, fight, and pray.
I'm going to watch, fight, and pray.
I'm going to watch, fight, and pray until I die!

I'm going to see my family saved.
I'm going to see my family saved.
I'm going to see my family saved **before** I die!
I'm going to see my family saved.
I'm going to see my family saved.
I'm going to see my family saved **before** I die!

*"Soldiers fight not because they hate what is in front of them, but because they love what is behind them."* There's an entire generation coming behind you. Fight because you love that they are walking behind you.

(Photo Getty Images Zabelin)

# CHAPTER SEVEN

# LIVE LIKE YOU WERE DYING

*"The goal isn't to live forever; the goal is to fashion something that will."*

—*Fernando E. Franco Sr.*

In my first book, ***dis.con.tinued,*** I mentioned a dreadful experience about the day when my wife was diagnosed with Leukemia cancer. What is ironic about this chapter is I find myself writing it today on May 13, 2020. The same exact date that my wife was diagnosed 15 years ago with this life thunderous disease!

Friday the 13th May of 2005 was a real eye-opener for me confronting the reality of death. The news was not good! Her diagnosis was so sudden, without any warnings or symptoms whatsoever. On Thursday, she was perfectly healthy (So we thought). By Friday, she was diagnosed with the last stage of Chronic Myeloid Leukemia!

There are three stages of Chronic Myeloid Leukemia (CML)

- **Chronic:** This is the earliest phase of CML. The majority of CML patients are diagnosed during this phase as a result of mild symptoms, particularly fatigue.
- **Accelerated:** If CML has not responded to treatment well during the chronic phase, it becomes more aggressive, which can lead to the accelerated phase. At this point, symptoms may become more noticeable.
- **Blastic:** This is the most aggressive stage of chronic myeloid leukemia. Blastic refers to having more than 20 percent myeloblasts or lymphoblasts.

My wife and I had no idea whatsoever that she was sick with CML. We were told that Friday that she was at the blastic stage of CML with a white blood count of 380,000 and a blast count of 31 percent.

Fast-forwarding ten years after her diagnosis, we celebrated an enormous ten-year cancer-free festivity at our church. I asked her oncologist if he can write a summary of his take on what happened on Friday the 13th of the year 2005.

## The summary in part reads:

*I met Veronica for the first time at St. John's Medical Center in Oxnard about 7 P.M. on May 13, 2005. I was on my way home to Los Angeles on the Ventura Freeway when I was called about this 31-year-old woman who was six weeks pregnant. She had 380,000 white blood cell count with 31% blast cell, which indicated active leukemia. Normal white blood cell count is about 5,000.*

My wife, Veronica's white blood count was 76 times higher than the normal person. Her oncologist, that day in the Emergency Room, said, "I don't know how you are still alive. You should have at least died from a heart attack."

We had a reason to celebrate ten years later. With nearly 700 in attendance at the celebration, she was filled with many surprises, love, and applause that she so well deserved for her towering fight. We laughed, cried, and gave God all the glory for her healing, and continually exercise up until this day.

One of the surprises at her celebration was when I sang her the song (*Live like You Were Dyin'* by Tim McGraw) live on stage.

### Live Like You Were Dyin'
### By: Tim McGraw

She said: "I was in my early thirties,
"With a lot of life before me,
And a moment came that stopped me on a dime.
"I spent most of the next days,
"Looking at the x-rays,
And talking bout the options and talkin 'bout sweet time."
I asked him when it sank in, that
this might really be the real end?
How's it hit you when you get that kind of news?
Man whatcha do?

An' he said: "I went sky diving, I went rocky mountain climbing,
"I went two point seven seconds on a bull named Fu Man Chu.
"And I loved deeper and I spoke sweeter,
"And I gave forgiveness I'd been denying."
An' he said: "Someday, I hope you get the chance,
"To live like you were dyin'."

"I was finally the husband,
"That most the time I wasn't.
I became a friend a friend would like to have.
"All a sudden goin' fishin',
"Wasn't such an imposition,
"And I went three times that year I lost my Dad.
I finally read the Good Book,
"And I took a good long hard look,
"At what I'd do if I could do it all again,
"And then:

"I went sky diving, I went rocky mountain climbing,
"I went two point seven seconds on a bull named Fu Man Chu.
"And I loved deeper and I spoke sweeter,
"And I gave forgiveness I'd been denying."
An' he said: "Someday, I hope you get the chance,
"To live like you were dyin'."

**I FOUND THAT ONE OF THE WAYS TO RECOVER IS TO LIVE LIKE YOU WERE DYING.** This book you are reading is about the pain and recovery of a pastor. I hope that it has given you an insight into how to recover from pain. I found that one of the ways to recover is to live like you were dying. The honest truth about life is that it is not forever; the goal is to fashion something that will last forever during our short stay on earth.

As a pastor, I have buried a lot more people than I have married. I have put to rest, bodies from the ages of just months old, seven years old, seventy, and so on. Each time at the funeral service, I am reminded that there are a lot of things that you borrow in life, but one thing you can't borrow is tomorrow. You can't borrow tomorrow.

**YOU CAN'T BORROW TOMORROW.**

If you're from the old school, then your mom perhaps sent you to borrow a cup of milk or a scoop of sugar from the next-door neighbor. What is awesome about that truth is that neighbors would actually give it.

The local convenient markets and lunch trucks at job sites would allow you to have a tab with them and pay them at the end of the week. Obviously, this was before the credit card system was in existence.

Jesus said:

> *Give to the one who asks you, and do not turn away from the one who wants to <u>borrow</u> from you.*

King Solomon says:

> *Do not say to your neighbor, "Come back tomorrow and I'll give it to you"—when you already have it with you* (**Proverbs 3:28**).

I know that the word *borrow* has a bad taste to it, and the Bible even says that one day we will be the lender and not the borrower. But the truth is, there are times that we will and may have to borrow for certain seasons that we find life puts us in, or in some cases, we put ourselves in.

A lot of people detest the word *borrow*, but even Jesus borrowed while He was here on earth. It's interesting to find that Jesus came into this world and left the same, with things having to be borrowed for Him.

## THINGS BORROWED BY JESUS AND FOR JESUS:

### 1. A BORROWED STABLE/MANGER

**Luke 2:6, 7**

> *And so, it was, that, while they were there, the days were accomplished that she should be delivered. And she brought forth her firstborn son, and wrapped him in swaddling clothes, and laid him in a manger; because there was no room for them in the inn.*

Part of the Christmas song, "Away in a Manger," that is sung all across the world, says, "Away in a manger no crib for a bed / The little lord Jesus laid down his sweet head." This song was inspired by a single verse in the Bible.

The place He was born in was a manger; it was a borrowed space where cattle are fed, and He was laid *in that manger* instead of a cradle. From the time He was born until He died, this world had no room for Jesus.

## 2. A BORROWED BOAT

Luke 5:3

> *He got into one of the boats, the one belonging to Simon, and asked him to put out a little from shore. Then he sat down and taught the people from the boat.*

Simon Peter should have known from day one that to be a disciple of Christ, a lot of giving was going to be involved in following Jesus, including his own life one day.

Jesus immediately borrowed a boat and made it His pulpit.

## 3. BORROWED LOAVES & FISH

John 6:8-11

> *Another of his disciples, Andrew, Simon Peter's brother, spoke up, "Here is a boy with five small barley loaves and two small fish, but how far will they go among so many?"*

> *Jesus said, "Have the people sit down." There was*
> *plenty of grass in that place, and they sat down*
> *(about five thousand men were there). Jesus then*
> *took the loaves, gave thanks, and distributed to those*
> *who were seated as much as they wanted. He did the*
> *same with the fish.*

**DON'T WORRY ABOUT PUTTING IT TOGETHER; JUST GET IT TOGETHER.**

While the disciples wanted to **give up**, Jesus was ready to **give out**. We, as His disciples, are distributors, not manufacturers.

Don't worry about putting it together; just get it together. Jesus knows how to multiply what He borrows.

## 4. A BORROWED DONKEY

**Matthew 21:1-3**

> *As they approached Jerusalem and came to*
> *Bethphage on the Mount of Olives, Jesus sent two*
> *disciples, saying to them, "Go to the village ahead of*
> *you, and at once you will find a donkey tied there,*
> *with her colt by her. Untie them and bring them to*
> *me. If anyone says anything to you, say that the Lord*
> *needs them, and he will send them right away.*

It's amazing what Jesus can use to get all the glory. Jesus could have ridden on a stallion, but the horse would have stolen the glory! This is why Jesus uses simple people, so we can make sure He receives all the glory.

## 5. A BORROWED ROOM

Mark 14:12-15

> On the first day of the Festival of Unleavened Bread,
> when it was customary to sacrifice the Passover lamb,
> Jesus' disciples asked him, "Where do you want us to
> go and make preparations for you to eat the Passover?"
>
> So, he sent two of his disciples, telling them, "Go into
> the city, and a man carrying a jar of water will meet
> you. Follow him. Say to the owner of the house he
> enters, 'The Teacher asks: Where is my guest room,
> where I may eat the Passover with my disciples?' He
> will show you a large room upstairs, furnished and
> ready. Make preparations for us there."

When Jesus was born, He didn't have His own room. Now, at His last supper, He did not even have His own dinner table. It's a borrowed dinner room with borrowed furnishings for His very last meal with His disciples.

We must understand that this was the first Airbnb that ever existed. Many people in Jerusalem would rent their rooms out for people who were traveling there for the "Passover."

This owner did not charge Jesus but allowed Him to borrow the room.

## 6. A BORROWED TOMB

Luke 23:50-56

> *Now there was a man named Joseph, a member of the Council, a good and upright man, who had not consented to their decision and action. He came from the Judean town of Arimathea, and he himself was waiting for the kingdom of God. Going to Pilate, he asked for Jesus' body.*

> *Then he took it down, wrapped it in linen cloth and placed it in a tomb cut in the rock, one in which no one had yet been laid.*

Who knows who this man, Joseph, was saving this tomb for? Himself, family? Not too sure. However, it really didn't matter because it would be made available again just three days later!

We need to live like we were dying tomorrow. This life is brief—we are all just passing through. You may have the opinion today, "I don't believe in borrowing; I'll never borrow, that's not me." The truth of it all is; we are all borrowing one thing—LIFE.

Paul the apostle said to the Corinthians:

2 Corinthians 5:1

> *For we know that if the earthly tent we live in is destroyed, we have a building from God, an eternal house in heaven, not built by human hands.*

We all are just living in borrowed tents that our souls occupy.

There is something that you have, and then there is something that you don't have.

1. **What you have with you = It's called TODAY**
2. **What you don't have with you = TOMORROW**

Research shows us that 151,000 people die each day. Tomorrow is not promised.

**RESEARCH SHOWS US THAT 151,000 PEOPLE DIE EACH DAY.**

One thing about Jesus borrowing things was that He returned them in better condition!

The psalmist made it clear to us that we ought to live like we were dying when he said:

**Psalm 39:4**

> *Lord, remind me how brief my time on earth will be. Remind me that my days are numbered, and that my life is fleeing away.*

We also find in the Book of Job the fact that we were born only yesterday and know nothing, and our days on earth are but a shadow.

The Bible uses terms like alien, pilgrim, foreigner, stranger, and visitor.

David said:

**Psalm 119:19**

> *I am but a foreigner here on earth.*

Peter confirmed this truth:

**1 Peter 1:17**

> *If you call God your father, live your time as temporary residents on earth.*

God says that His children are to think differently about life from the way unbelievers do.

**Philippians 3:20**

> *But our citizenship is in heaven. And we eagerly await a Savior from there, the Lord Jesus Christ.*

**1 Peter 2:11**

> *Friends, this world is not your home, so don't make yourselves cozy in it. Don't indulge your ego at the expense of your soul.*

**1 Corinthians 7:31**

*Those in frequent contact with the things of the world should make good use of them without becoming attached to them, for this world and all it contains will pass away.*

Three buddies were discussing death, and one asked the group: "What would you like people to say about you at your funeral?" One said: "He was a great humanitarian, who cared about his community." Another said: "He was a great husband and father, who was an example for many to follow." The third said: "I'd like people to say, 'Look, he's moving!!'"

The above illustration may sound funny, but the truth is, once we take our last breath here on earth, it is to be present with the Lord. So, as long as you are still here, live like you are dying because every day, we are.

**SO, AS LONG AS YOU ARE STILL HERE, LIVE LIKE YOU ARE DYING BECAUSE EVERY DAY, WE ARE.**

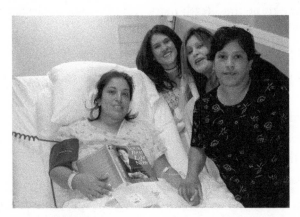

(My wife Veronica at U.C.L.A. hospital with Lukemia Cancer. Pictured with Veronica's sisters Yolanda, Irene and Sophia.)

# CHAPTER EIGHT

# ASHES IN THE WIND

*"You have to die inside to rise from your own ashes."*

—*Fernando E. Franco Sr.*

In some churches, during the first day of what they call Lent, many people around the world walk in and out of churches with what they believe to be the "death mark" upon their foreheads.

It's simply ashes mixed with oil applied in the shape of a cross, what is known to them as "Ash Wednesday."

The word "Lent" comes from the Old English word, *"lencten,"* which means "spring." Pretty much what some would call a spring cleaning in their lives.

The ashes on the forehead represent the death of our Savior on the cross. But why the forehead?

Mary poured this ointment on Jesus' head, and Jesus tells His disciples that she did this because it was in preparation for His burial.

At burials, in ancient Israel, a king's body is anointed; the same goes for a priest. In the case of Jesus, He explained that she anointed Him for **His** *burial*. What the disciples called a waste, Jesus called it beautiful.

The ashes supposedly and traditionally are made from the burned palms of the last year's Palm Sunday.

Don't get confused by why some people wear it on their foreheads. They don't wear ashes to proclaim their holiness but to acknowledge that they are sinners.

## WHAT THE ASHES SYMBOLIZE IN THE BIBLE

- ✓ Repentance
- ✓ Humility
- ✓ Mortality

The ashes not only represent the death of Christ, but it also represents our death—our daily spiritual death to *self*, and the physical death that we will all face one day.

We were created from the dust, and to the dust (ashes) we shall return.

You may have heard of the term, *sackcloth and ashes*. This term refers to the ancient Hebrew custom of indicating humility before God by wearing a coarse cloth, commonly used to make sacks, and dusting oneself with ashes.

Jesus used this term in Matthew chapter eleven when He started to preach hard to the remorseless cities.

**Matthew 11:20-24**

> *Then He began to rebuke the cities in which most of His mighty works had been done, because they did not repent: "Woe to you, Chorazin! Woe to you, Bethsaida! For if the mighty works which were done in you had been done in Tyre and Sidon, they would have repented long ago in* **sackcloth and ashes.**

Sackcloth and ashes were worn to publicly express or show sorrow or regret for having done something wrong with an apology.

Okay, so maybe you did something wrong that is keeping your life on pause. Simply repent, throw off the sackcloth, dust off the ashes and rev up your engine because God is not through with you. God does not despise a broken spirit and a contrite heart. Man will always look at the outer appearance, but God always looks at the heart. Don't let anyone tell you where your heart is at with God. People could only assume but they are not God. Even a man of God is not God. Nobody knows your heart like God does. Again, a broken spirit and a contrite heart God will not despise.

1.  Brokenness helps us to handle the blessings of God safely.
2.  Brokenness helps us to discover God's strength.
3.  Brokenness makes us more like Jesus.

## 16 PEOPLE THAT JESUS TOUCHED WITH A BROKEN SPIRIT AND A CONTRITE HEART

1.  A despised tax collector.
    Matthew 9:9

2.  An insane hermit.
    Mark 5:1-6

3.  A Roman Governor.
    John 18:38

4.  A religious leader.
    John 3:1-2

5.  A homemaker.
    Luke 10:38-40

6.  A King.
    Luke 23:7-11

7.  A criminal.
    Luke 23:40-43

8.  A poor widow.
    Luke 7:11

9. **A Roman Captain.**
   Luke 7:1-10

10. **A prophet.**
    Matthew 3:13-15

11. **An adulterous woman.**
    John 8:1-11

12. **A rich man.**
    Mark 10:17-23

13. **A beggar.**
    Mark 10:46-52

14. **An outcast with leprosy.**
    Luke 17:11-19

15. **An enemy who hated Him.**
    Acts 9:1-9

16. **A traitor.**
    John 13:1-2

## ASHES IN THE WIND

You have to die inside to rise from your own ashes and believe that God will give you a crown of beauty for those same ashes.

I declare over your life, not only for you to be raised out of your dust, but for you to be made to look pleasant and become a great ornament to your profession. I declare over your life that your garments of sackcloth will be exchanged for the garments of praise. The beautiful garments that were worn on thanksgiving days in the Bible shall you wear every day of your life.

One thing I know for sure, you cannot praise God and remain defeated at the same time. Sometimes, you won't feel like doing it, and you won't feel like having the right attitude. You may not even feel like being grateful. This is why God says we should offer up the sacrifice of praise.

**YOU CANNOT PRAISE GOD AND REMAIN DEFEATED AT THE SAME TIME.**

OFFER UP – NOT DOWN! It's easier to drop something than it is to LIFT something up. Some of you will need to learn how to praise God all by yourself. You have to praise God through a lot of tears and have to lay your own hands on your head to come up from your ashes.

So, tilt your chin up, pull your shoulder out, and lift up the name of Jesus Christ with the sacrifice of praise.

When you put on the garment of praise, the ashes must blow away by the wind of the Holy Spirit.

**WHEN YOU PUT ON THE GARMENT OF PRAISE, THE ASHES MUST BLOW AWAY BY THE WIND OF THE HOLY SPIRIT.**

*There was a father that had three very active boys, maybe some of you reading here know what that's like. And one summer evening, dad was out playing cops and robbers with his three boys in the backyard after dinner.*

*One of the boys "shot" his father and yelled, "Bang! You're dead!"*

*He slumped to the ground, and when he didn't get up right away, a neighbor ran over to see if he was okay. When the neighbor bent over and asked the dad, "Are you okay?"*

*The overworked father opened one eye and said, "Shhh. Don't give me away. This is the only chance I've had to rest all day long."*

Your rest is over! Press play and let the motor kick-start. You got this!

You may have been held under in life, but now, you're going to be coming over. You may have been forgotten, but now, you're remembered. You may have been oppressed, but now, you'll be blessed. You're going from rejected to accepted. From *heads were down* to being *lifted up*. What has been taken from you will be given back in a better way than it was taken.

Your ashes are in the wind. Put on your crowns. It's time to change your clothes.

(Man dressed in Sackcloth and Ashes on the
Ponte San Angelo photo by GOC53 on Flickr.)

# CHAPTER NINE

# THE DAY I KNOCKED OUT THE DEVIL

*"Satan caught me with my head down and got excited until I looked up and recited."*

—*Fernando E. Franco, Sr.*

S atan is real!

**JESUS** - would testify about a real devil at His temptation.

**PAUL** - testified that it was Satan that prevented him from returning to Thessalonica.

**THE ARCHANGEL MICHAEL** - contended with Satan over the body of Moses.

**PETER** - was sifted by Satan.

**ADAM & EVE** - were deceived by Satan.

**JUDAS** - hung himself when possesed by Satan.

**MANY OF YOU** - are encountering Satan this very moment as you read my book.

Someone once asked Evangelist Billy Sunday, *"Why do you believe in a real Devil?"* Billy replied, *"The Bible declares it to be so, and furthermore, I have done business with him myself."*

I must say that I can relate to what Evangelist Billy Sunday said. As for me, *Satan caught me with my head down and got excited until I looked up and recited.* You may ask, recited what? God's word! This is the only antidote we were given to defeat Satan.

I remember the day I knocked out the devil. I was thinking, *should I do it or should I not? Do what,* you may ask? Should I stop living or should I *con.tinue* living? If you read my book *dis.con.tinued,* then you know very well my detailed personal encounter with Satan himself in chapter two—Hater-isim.

I remember clearly the day Satan visited me in a hotel room. The temptation was real. I never felt the presence of Satan like I did that day on the 3$^{rd}$ story floor of that hotel. It was historical, as real as you can get on a one-on-one fight. My church wasn't present, no worship team, no pastors, and no one on the other line to help. It was just the devil and me. I'm sure God was there in the background because He never leaves us nor forsakes us. All God was waiting on was for me to call on His name and to quote the antidote. **Get thee behind me Satan!**

Even that was not the grand slam, because all Satan did was get behind me. Demons tremble at the name of Jesus, but Satan just takes a step behind you. And from behind you, he continues to talk, breathe his fiery breath down the backside of your neck and causes you to go into a moment of formidable sweat, high fever, and a panic full of anxiety. At least, that's what happened to me on this day!

**DEMONS TREMBLE AT THE NAME OF JESUS, BUT SATAN JUST TAKES A STEP BEHIND YOU.**

Although my wife was in the next room beside me (we were blessed with a penthouse suite this day by family), for some reason, I couldn't get the words out of my mouth to call on her for assistance. Even when Jesus had His encounter with Satan to jump and commit suicide, each time Jesus rebuked Satan, and after the third temptation, He is ministered to by angels. I'm not sure if angels came to my rescue, but I know that I'm still alive, throwing punches, having victories, and writing this book.

In that hotel room, it was a gruesome war between Satan and me. I was crying out of fear and crying out the name of Jesus simultaneously. I was shivering and focused at the same time. I was cold and hot at the same time. I was afraid and comforted at the same time. I can't even explain the reality of the event.

I couldn't see Satan, but I could feel him and hear him. His voice was just as loud as his presence. This was something different.

I've been warring in the heavenlies for countless of years, but this time, it seemed as if the war was taking place right here on earth, in a hotel room in sunny California. Satan is real and so is his voice.

## NBC'S—THE VOICE

The show's innovative format features four stages of competition:

1. The blind auditions.
2. The battle rounds.
3. The knockouts.
4. The live performance shows.

During the blind auditions, the decisions from the musician coaches are based solely on voice and not on looks. The coaches hear the artists perform, but they don't get to see them. However, their rotating chairs allow them to turn and see the contestant. If a coach is impressed by the artist's voice, he/she pushes the big red button on their chair to select the artist for his/her team.

Once the teams are set, the battle is on. After the vocal battle, the coach must choose which of his/her singers will advance to the next rounds of competition.

In the final live performance phase of the competition, the top artists from each team will compete each week against each other during a live broadcast.

In the end, one will be named "**The Voice**" and will receive the grand prize of cash and a recording contract.

**SATAN'S VOICE IS SO MUCH MORE INFLUENTIAL THAN HIS LOOKS.**

Satan's voice is so much more influential than his looks. Actually, you'll rarely see Satan but we will hear him often.

# SATAN'S VOICE

*Which voice do you listen to?* We are told very clearly what Satan's voice sounds like in the Book of Romans in the Bible.

**Romans 8:1**

> **"Therefore, there is now no condemnation for those who are in Christ Jesus..."**

Later on, in chapter eight, it talks about those who do not live according to the flesh but according to the Spirit. Those who live according to the Spirit have their minds set on what the Spirit desires.

When someone makes mistakes, if they are in the flesh, they beat themselves up. They feel GUILTY and UNWORTHY. They live DOUBTFUL, DEPRESSED, and DEFEATED. When someone chooses that response, they usually end up on a dead-end street.

Too many people go around feeling bad about themselves. When they make mistakes, instead of receiving God's mercy and moving forward, they listen to the wrong voice.

## THE VOICE OF THE ACCUSER

This voice constantly rails at you about your,

*Mistakes*
*Bad habits*
*Temper tantrums*
*Shortcomings*

After so long of hearing an accuser in your head, you get weighed down, actually believing the accusations.

An accusation is a charge or claim that someone has done something illegal or wrong. What we have to remind the devil every day is that the reason Jesus Christ died for you is for your wrongs to be forgiven.

## THE VOICE OF THE GUILT

Someone once said,

> *"Guilt puts you on a treadmill. You're constantly working and struggling and sweating, but you still don't move forward."*

The voice of guilt and self-condemnation makes it difficult to think important of yourself, your family, and the general public.

<u>What the burden of guilt does to a person:</u>

*It drains your strength, energy, and enthusiasm.*
*It will prevent you from forming healthy relationships.*
*It can affect you not only emotionally but physically.*

There have been so many people that have suffered nervous breakdowns because of guilt. Year after year, they have carried the heaviness. They are worn down and can barely function.

## THE VOICE THAT TELLS LIES

**THERE HAVE BEEN SO MANY PEOPLE THAT HAVE SUFFERED NERVOUS BREAKDOWNS BECAUSE OF GUILT. YEAR AFTER YEAR, THEY HAVE CARRIED THE HEAVINESS. THEY ARE WORN DOWN AND CAN BARELY FUNCTION.**

Yes, Satan is indeed a defeated foe, but he is a deceiver! Satan's lies have always resulted in *five ways* since he lied while crawling in the Garden of Eden. He is a masquerade and also excellent at it. For God's sake, his very first try worked while dialoguing in the Garden as a serpent. Most people I know run away from snakes, but the devil this day must have masqueraded himself pretty darn good.

### Doubt

The devil makes you question God's word and His goodness.

## Discouragement

The devil makes you look at the size of your problems rather than the size of your God.

## Diversion

The devil makes the wrong things seem attractive so that you will want them more than the right things.

## Defeat

The devil makes you feel like a failure so that you don't even try anymore.

## Delay

The devil makes you put off doing something so that it never gets done.

I've gotten to know Satan really well over the years, not because I choose to spend time with him, but because God permits him to visit me. I find his visitations a compliment from God. Just as he allowed the devil to visit some of God's greatest servants, I find it a privilege to be considered.

# WHEN THE WAR AIN'T FAIR—IT'S WARFARE

**THE DEVIL DOES NOT PLAY FAIR. HE'S A CHEATER, LIAR, AND TWO-FACED. DO NOT TRUST HIM!**

The devil does not play fair. He's a cheater, liar, and two-faced. Do not trust him! We have the authority to move Satan behind us, under us, and away from us.

We have what is called delegated authority. Just like a police officer has been given delegated authority to arrest someone, we have been given delegated authority to tell Satan what to do.

**Matthew 28:18-20**

> *Then Jesus came to them and said, "All authority in heaven and on earth has been given to me. Therefore go and make disciples of all nations, baptizing them in the name of the Father and of the Son and of the Holy Spirit, and teaching them to obey everything I have commanded you. And surely I am with you always, to the very end of the age."*

Jesus has been given ALL authority, and He commands us to go *IN* His authority and *WITH* His authority! We got to go IN IT and WITH IT!

When you step into warfare, you are going *in with it!* The authority we have is not ours but it has been one that has been delegated to you by Him. My power is useless; your authority is futile.

The Bible says that Man's greatest strength is God's weakness. The authority has been delegated to us, and it is not ours but HIS.

*When and if you have a problem with a service at a restaurant, you demand to see the manager of that restaurant. Why? The manager has been given the delegated authority from the owner of that restaurant.*

We ask for the person **"In Charge,"** the person with **"authority."** When God created this world, He intended for mankind to be **"In Charge"** of it!

**Genesis 1:26**

> *Then God said, "Let us make mankind in our image, in our likeness, so that they may rule over the fish in the sea and the birds in the sky, over the livestock and all the wild animals, and over all the creatures that move along the ground."*

Have you ever considered the fact that you were created to rule the earth? From the beginning, God set apart the world as our domain.

**Psalm 115:16**

> *The highest heavens belong to the LORD, but the earth he has given to mankind.*

When God created Adam, He told him to FILL and SUBDUE the earth. Subdue means to conquer, or to bring under subjection.

I remember before I became the lead pastor of my church, my pastor had taken a sabbatical before his resignation and told me that I was in charge while he was away. At that time, I was somewhat in charge, but when he was away, I realized that now I was fully in charge. I had to make crucial decisions on my own! I had to approve or disapprove budgets. I had to preach every week, not just occasionally. I had to answer the tough questions and give tough answers.

**SOMETIMES, GOD DON'T ANSWER HIS PHONE ON PURPOSE. HE'S FORCING YOU TO USE YOUR AUTHORITY THAT HE HAD ALREADY DELEGATED!**

I would call his cell phone plenty of times because I didn't want to make a mistake or follow the wrong decision. He didn't answer his phone on his sabbatical, and I was forced to use my authority.

Sometimes, God don't answer His phone on purpose. He's forcing you to USE YOUR AUTHORITY that He had already delegated!

This is what I used to knock out the devil in that hotel room that day. I used the delegated authority that was given to me. It seemed as if God wasn't answering His phone on the greatest test day in my life. But I had all the answers to the test and just used what I had already known. I knew that Greater is HE that is in me than he that is in this world!

Jesus said:

**Luke 10:19**

> *I have given you authority to trample on snakes and scorpions and to overcome all the power of the enemy; nothing will harm you.*

Knowing that we have power and not using it will accomplish nothing; we need to know what belongs to us. We need to know that we have AUTHORITY OVER demonic forces.

You have AUTHORITY OVER...

1. Smoking
2. Cheating
3. Cussing
4. Lying
5. Drug addiction
6. Strongholds and bad habits
7. Poverty
8. Demonic Powers

## DECLARE YOUR RIGHTS AND USE THOSE KEYS

Jesus said:

**Matthew 16:19**

> *And I will give to you the keys of the kingdom of heaven: and whatever you shall bind on earth shall be bound in heaven: and whatever you shall loose on earth shall be loosed in heaven.*

Declare what Jesus has already done. Jesus has suffered in my place. Paul the Apostle wrote:

**Romans 16:20**

> *And the God of peace shall bruise Satan under your*
> *feet...*

This single verse is talking to those who are tired of the devil blocking their way and causing all kinds of problems. How would you like to lift your foot as high as you can and then slam it down as hard as you can with the devil underneath your feet?

The word, *bruise*, in Greek, is pronounced **Suntribo.** This word was historically used to denote the act of smashing grapes into wine. It was used literally as a word that means being extremely crushed, that in the end, it gives us a picture of the object being so crushed that it would be beyond recognition.

When you and I use the word *suntribo* on Satan, we move from being defeated to,

1. Pounding Satan
2. Hammering Satan
3. Trampling Satan
4. Smattering Satan
5. Obliterating Satan
6. Smashing Satan
7. Trouncing Satan
8. Bruising Satan
9. Crushing Satan
10. Demolishing Satan BEYOND RECOGNITION!

The word *shortly* comes from a military term that described the way Roman Soldiers marched in formation. When the Roman soldiers would march, they would do so with determination and perseverance. They would move forward with marching orders that if anyone tried to interfere or hinder them, they were to keep walking.

Even innocent bystanders, who might fall into their path, were not to be pitied. They stopped for nothing!

Worse yet, the Roman soldiers had spikes on their feet, meant to secure their step on all terrain—groundbreakers. If you got in their way, you were as good as dead. You would be struck down and trampled on without mercy.

You see, Jesus has already crushed the head of the enemy. Satan is defeated! We are simply taking sure steps, treading in a path well laid by our Savior, Jesus Christ. He has ordered our steps.

We are not doormats in the Devil's kingdom. We are warriors in God's kingdom.

**WE ARE NOT DOORMATS IN THE DEVIL'S KINGDOM. WE ARE WARRIORS IN GOD'S KINGDOM.**

Go ahead and Give it a try as you finish this chapter. Do what I did. Let today be the day that you knock out the devil!

*As an old farmer was driving down the freeway, his cell phone rang. Answering, he heard his wife's voice urgently warning him, "Bill, I just heard on the news that there's a car going the wrong way on Highway*

*59. Please, be careful!" "Honey," Bill replied, "It's not just one car. It's hundreds of them!"*

Just get off the wrong road, get back on track, and knock out Satan.

I must warn you. He'll get back up again for another round. Just enjoy your time while he is out for the count. But one day, he'll be defeated once and for all.

(Photo wbur.org)

# CHAPTER TEN

# MY DREAM WON'T
# LET ME GIVE UP!

*"In my life, I will admit that I have quit multiple times, but I never really did give up. I have quit but rose each time more passionate to just try again."*

—Fernando E. Franco, Sr.

I have a dream; you have a dream; we all have a dream. We started dreaming as children. Little boys want to be a firefighter and little girls want to be a nurse. Children pick up dreams early on. They just don't know what the dream will demand at their young age.

Dreams are just that—a dream! Dreams don't become the real world until we put our all on the dream. The brutal truth about a dream is that we will want to give up once the opponents come in waves. Every dream has an opponent.

**DREAMS DON'T BECOME THE REAL WORLD UNTIL WE PUT OUR ALL ON THE DREAM.**

"Pain is temporary. Quitting lasts forever."
*Lance Armstrong*

"Age wrinkles the body. Quitting wrinkles, the soul."
*Douglas Macarthur*

"If you quit once it becomes a habit. Never quit."
*Michael Jordan*

I think that at one time or another, we all may have quit but didn't give up. We quit in our minds, we quit for a season, we quit on the inside, but the dream don't let us give up.

At the age of 16 years old, I knew I wanted to be a pastor. At age 18, God confirmed I would be a pastor. At the age of 25, I became a pastor. The truth is, I didn't know that the process of becoming a pastor would be much easier than the fight to remain a pastor itself! This may not be the case for every pastor, but it has been the case for me.

**AS LONG AS YOU ARE INHALING AND EXHALING, IT'S NOT TOO LATE TO START DREAMING AGAIN. PUT BACK ON THOSE OVERALLS.**

You may be reading this book right now, and possibly you have quit and given up, but as long as you are inhaling and exhaling, it's not too late to start dreaming again. Put back on those overalls. You may have had a life interruption, but it doesn't mean that you should live an interrupted life. Carry on! The pause is over.

**YOU MAY HAVE HAD A LIFE INTERRUPTION, BUT IT DOESN'T MEAN THAT YOU SHOULD LIVE AN INTERRUPTED LIFE**

# RELIGION CAN BE A ROADBLOCK TO HAPPINESS

In 1938, 73% of Americans were church attenders. Today, less than 50% of Americans attend church. Why is that? People are "SICK OF RELIGION," sick of being controlled, sick of being judged, and sick of fake love.

I don't ever want to have to go to church or to serve God because I'm being controlled to do so. God was so against it from day one. This is why He gave Adam and Eve the free will to choose if they would eat or not eat from the tree of the knowledge of good and evil. God does not control you. He is just in control. I want to go to church because I can't wait to be part of the church, see my church, and touch the church. When people start going to church because they want to and not because they are forced to, that era marks the season when churches will start having revivals. We won't be able to help but to start taking people to church with us, so they can have the same experiences with God that we are having!

**GOD DOES NOT CONTROL YOU. HE IS JUST IN CONTROL.**

It was the love, miracles, and sacrifice that Jesus modeled that attracted and converted the weary generation of religious folks in His day. Today, it's still the same remedy that will knock down the roadblock to happiness.

**LOVE
MIRACLES
SACRIFICE**

Jesus was good in the methodology of how to attract crowds, but that was not what brought forth the transformation to happiness.

Think about it. Jesus…

1. Preached from a boat.
2. Healed the man lowered through a roof.
3. Fed 5000 people through supernatural multiplication.

Jesus knew how to attract crowds. The front door to the church is quite easy. Just do some fancy stuff, and you'll get a crowd. It's closing the back door to a church that is always the challenging task for a church. Attracting them is easy, but keeping them is hard.

Jesus' largest crowd that He ever attracted was through "His Death." – Love always wins! The sacrificial death was the biggest attraction of His ministry.

**John 3:1-2**

> *"Now there was a Pharisee, a man named Nicodemus who was a member of the Jewish ruling council. He came to Jesus at night and said, "Rabbi, we know that you are a teacher who has come from God. For no one could perform the signs you are doing if God were not with him."*

Nicodemus was part of the Pharisees—a member of the Jewish ruling council (perhaps the teachers of the Law). He had already seen that Jesus was more than just a law. He was love.

Being loved, expressing love, and living a lifestyle that loves is what will always bring happiness, not religion.

> **BEING LOVED, EXPRESSING LOVE, AND LIVING A LIFESTYLE THAT LOVES IS WHAT WILL ALWAYS BRING HAPPINESS, NOT RELIGION.**

## RELIGION CAN MAKE YOU GIVE UP

Just about ten years before the birth of Jesus, the Roman senate had passed a law that read, "In any conquered province within the Roman Empire, soldiers may compel able-bodied men to bear their cargo one mile, but no more."

If a Roman soldier saw a Jewish man or boy, he could order the person by law to carry his cargo or burden for a mile. *(It's been said that every Jewish boy had a mile marked off in his head from every direction from the doorstep of his house).*

The Jewish boy or man was required by law to carry this soldier's burden for up to one mile. However, most Jews would not carry this backpack one inch or one foot further than the law required.

The Roman mile was 1,520 yards, just a bit shorter than the American mile.

As you can imagine, this law caused terrible resentment among the Jews toward the Roman government. Can you imagine how the Jews felt when Jesus said, *"Go the second mile?"*

**Matthew 5:41**

> *If anyone forces you to go one mile, go with them two miles.*

I'm sure people said, "Jesus is kidding, right? Does he really expect us to do more than the law requires us to do?" In essence, what Jesus was saying is that "my disciples" need to do more than the legalists and religious who do no more than what is only required of them!

## THE DIFFERENCE BETWEEN THE FIRST MILE AND THE SECOND MILE:

The first mile is **RELIGION**
The second mile is **RELATIONSHIP**

Jesus came to break the curse of RELIGION. For some religious people in the Bible, it upset them, and for others, it attracted them.

Being religious will make you give up. But when you are hanging out with Jesus, there is never anything religious about Him. Therefore, the more you are walking with Him, the less likely you are to give up. In fact, the only thing the disciples gave up because of their relationship with Jesus was their life—a martyr's death!

The Pharisees and all the other prominent and religious groups lived in the first mile. This is why they were not the ones who changed the world. Those who have a relationship with Jesus are the ones who changed the world.

As long as love is your driving force for your dream, you may quit here and there, but you won't give up!

**AS LONG AS LOVE IS YOUR DRIVING FORCE FOR YOUR DREAM, YOU MAY QUIT HERE AND THERE, BUT YOU WON'T GIVE UP!**

## THERE WERE A TOTAL OF SIX PROMINENT RELIGIONS AND POLITICAL GROUPS IN THE BIBLE:

1. PHARISEES
2. SADDUCEES
3. TEACHERS OF THE LAW
4. SUPPORTERS OF HEROD
5. ZEALOTS
6. ESSENS

Each one of these groups disagreed with Jesus! Religion has a type of control over people, and Jesus came to set the captives free! These six religious groups were in places of power and didn't want to lose their position of advantage.

### The Pharisees:

- "Were a strict group of religious Jews who advocated."
- "Very influential in the Synagogues."
- "Many of the Pharisees were also 'Teachers of the Law.'"

- "They Rejected Jesus' claim to be the Messiah. They despised Jesus because He didn't follow all their traditions, and He associated with notoriously wicked people."

## The Sadducees:

- "Were a wealthy, upper class, priestly party."
- "They profited from business in the Temple."
- "They only believed in the five books of Moses."
- "They rejected, denied, and disagreed with Jesus' resurrection from the dead."

## The Teachers of the Law:

- "They were professional interpreters of the Law."
- "They denied Jesus' authority to interpret the Law Himself because He did not obey all of their traditions. (Example: Healing someone on the Sabbath)."
- "Though He was the word in the flesh, He was rejected for interpreting the Law."

## Supporters of Herod:

- "They were a political party."
- "King Herod's supporters."
- "They tried to trap Jesus with questions and plotted to kill Him."
- "They saw Jesus as a threat to their political future at a time when they were trying to regain their political power from Rome."

## Zealots:

- "A fiercely dedicated group of Jewish loyalists determined to end Roman rule in Israel."
- "They believed in the Messiah but did not recognize Jesus as the Anointed One sent from God."
- "They believed that the Messiah was supposed to be a political leader who would deliver Israel from Roman authority."

## Essens:

- "They were a Jewish monastic group."
- "Monastic" = Somewhat like Monks that lived away from society and practiced the consecration of purity and extreme holiness."
- "They believed that their ceremonial rituals made them righteous, and not the teachings of Jesus and He being the final sacrifice to make a person right with God."

As mentioned, each of the six religious groups disagreed with Jesus, and to disagree with Jesus is to disagree with His love. And to disagree with His love could define a man as RELIGIOUS. It's religion that causes a man or woman to give up.

Nicodemus was tired of being around people who quoted the verse but

**NICODEMUS WAS TIRED OF BEING AROUND PEOPLE WHO QUOTED THE VERSE BUT DIDN'T REHEARSE THE VERSE. HE WAS TIRED OF BEING AROUND A GROUP THAT PREACHED THE LAW BUT DIDN'T PRACTICE IT.**

didn't rehearse the verse. He was tired of being around a group that preached the Law but didn't practice it.

The church, our country, your life, my life, needs to get sick of religion, and when we do, our dream won't let us give up.

## JESUS' DREAM DIDN'T LET HIM GIVE UP

Jesus' court trial was actually a series of hearings, carefully controlled to accomplish His death.

The verdict was predetermined, but certain "legal" procedures were necessary. A lot of effort went into condemning and executing an innocent man with a mission and dream to save the world.

**JESUS WENT THROUGH AN UNFAIR TRIAL IN OUR PLACE SO THAT WE WOULD NOT HAVE TO APPEAR IN OUR TRIAL WITH A GUILTY FACE.**

Jesus went through an unfair trial in our place so that we would not have to appear in our trial with a guilty face.

In no way at all were the religious leaders interested in giving Jesus a fair trial at all. In their minds, Jesus had to die. No ifs or buts. They had a blind obsession with killing Jesus that caused them to pervert the justice system they were appointed to protect.

# SIX REASONS WHY JESUS' TRIAL WAS ILLEGAL

## 1. EVEN BEFORE THE TRIAL HAD BEGAN, IT HAD BEEN DETERMINED THAT JESUS MUST DIE.

Mark 14:1

> *It was now two days before Passover and the Festival of Unleavened Bread. The leading priests and the teachers of religious law were still looking for an opportunity to capture Jesus secretly and kill him.*

There was "no innocent until proven guilty" approach, but that did not stop Jesus from pursuing His dream to save the world.

## 2. FALSE WITNESSES WERE SOUGHT TO TESTIFY AGAINST JESUS.

Usually, the religious leaders went through an elaborate system of screening witnesses to ensure justice. But not this time. That did not stop Jesus from pursuing His dream to save the world.

Matthew 26:59

> *Inside, the leading priests and the entire high council were trying to find witnesses who would lie about Jesus, so they could put him to death.*

## 3. NO DEFENSE FOR JESUS WAS SOUGHT OR EVEN ALLOWED.

Luke 22:67-71

> *"Tell us," they said, "are you the Messiah?" He answered, "If I tell you, you will not believe me; and if I ask you a question, you will not answer. But from now on the Son of Man will be seated at the right side of Almighty God. They all said, "Are you, then, the Son of God?"*
>
> *He answered them, "You say that I am."*
>
> *And they said, "We don't need any witnesses! We ourselves have heard what he said!"*

## 4. THE TRIAL WAS CONDUCTED AT NIGHT WHICH WAS ILLEGAL ACCORDING TO THE RELIGIOUS LEADERS' LAWS.

Mark 14:53-65

> *Jesus was led to the high priest's home where all of the chief priests and other Jewish leaders soon gathered. Peter followed far behind and then slipped inside the gates of the high priest's residence and crouched beside a fire among the servants.*
>
> *Inside, the chief priests and the whole Jewish Supreme Court were trying to find something against Jesus that would be sufficient to condemn him to death. But their efforts were in vain. Many false witnesses volunteered, but they contradicted each other.*

*Finally some men stood up to lie about him and said, "We heard him say, 'I will destroy this Temple made with human hands and in three days I will build another, made without human hands!'" But even then they didn't get their stories straight!*

*Then the high priest stood up before the Court and asked Jesus, "Do you refuse to answer this charge? What do you have to say for yourself?"*

*To this Jesus made no reply. Then the high priest asked him. "Are you the Messiah, the Son of God?" Jesus said, "I am, and you will see me[a]* sitting at the right hand of God, and returning to earth in the clouds of heaven."

*Then the high priest tore at his clothes and said, "What more do we need? Why wait for witnesses? You have heard his blasphemy. What is your verdict?" And the vote for the death sentence was unanimous. Then some of them began to spit at him, and they blindfolded him and began to hammer his face with their fists.*

*"Who hit you that time, you prophet?" they jeered. And even the bailiffs were using their fists on him as they led him away.*

## 5.  THE HIGH PRIEST PUT JESUS UNDER OATH BUT THEN INCRIMINATED HIM FOR WHAT HE SAID.

Matthew 26:63-66

> [63] *Then the high priest said to him, "I demand in the name of the living God that you tell us whether you claim to be the Messiah, the Son of God."*
>
> [64] *"Yes," Jesus said, "I am. And in the future you will see me, the Messiah,[a] sitting at the right hand of God and returning on the clouds of heaven."*
>
> [65-66] *Then the high priest tore at his own clothing, shouting, "Blasphemy! What need have we for other witnesses? You have all heard him say it! What is your verdict?"*
>
> *They shouted, "Death!—Death!—Death!"*

## 6.  CASES INVOLVING SUCH SERIOUS CHARGES WERE TO BE TRIED ONLY IN THE HIGH COUNCIL'S REGULAR MEETING PLACE, NOT IN THE HIGH PRIEST'S HOME.

Mark 14:53-64

> *Jesus was led to the high priest's home where all of the chief priests and other Jewish leaders soon gathered. Many false witnesses volunteered, but they contradicted each other.*
>
> *Then the high priest tore at his clothes and said, "What more do we need? Why wait for*

*witnesses? You have heard his blasphemy. What is
your verdict?" And the vote for the death sentence
was unanimous.*

None of these six reasons stopped Jesus in pursuing His dream to save the world.

Although Jesus' trial lasted less than 18 hours, He was taken to six different hearings. What court case that involves the verdict of execution have you ever heard of that only lasted 18 hours?

## Jesus had to go through TWO figures of AUTHORITIES.

1. Before the Jewish authorities
2. Before the Roman authorities.

### Three hearings before the Jewish authorities.

1st Hearing – Preliminary hearing before Annas

Because the office of the high priest was for life, Annas was still the "official" high priest in the eyes of the Jews.

2nd Hearing – Hearing before Caiaphas

Like the hearing before Annas, this hearing was conducted at night in secrecy. It was full of illegalities that made a mockery of the justice system.

### 3rd Hearing – Trial before the high council

Seventy members of the council met to rubber-stamp their approval of the previous hearing to make them appear legal. (Corruption in the church).

## Three hearings before the Roman authorities.

### 4th Hearing – First hearing before Pilate

The religious leaders had condemned Jesus to death on religious grounds, but ONLY the Roman Government could grant the death penalty.

Taking Him to the Governor, they accused Him of treason (a crime of betraying one's country, especially by attempting to overthrow the government). For such a crime as this, only the Roman Government could give the death penalty and not the Religious Leaders.

Pilate, the Governor, saw that Jesus was innocent, but was afraid of the uproar being caused by the religious leaders.

### 5th Hearing – Hearing before Herod

Because Jesus' home was in the region of Galilee, Pilate sent Jesus to Herod, the ruler of Galilee.

Herod was eager to see Jesus do a miracle, but when Jesus remained silent, Herod sent Him back to Pilate, the governor of the Roman province of Judea.

## 6th hearing – Last hearing before Pilate

On a personal note, Pilate didn't like the religious leaders. He wasn't interested in condemning the innocent man, Jesus!

However, he knew that another uprising in his district might cost him his job.

First, he tried to compromise with the religious leaders by having Jesus beaten, an illegal act in itself. But finally, he gave in and handed Jesus over to be executed.

Pilate's colors showed that self-interest was stronger than his sense of justice.

Jesus had a relationship with His father. When we choose a relationship over religion, nothing can get in our way. You may occasionally quit just like Jesus did when He was carrying His cross until Simon of Cyrene was ordered to carry Jesus' cross. But you will get back up again just like Jesus, take up your cross again, and will not give up. Why? Because your dream will not let you give up!

By now, I pray that the pause button is now your play button.

(Pastor Fernie embracing his dream. Broken people.)

# EPILOGUE

I wrote this book during the COVID-19 stay-at-home order. As of now, we have had two deaths of family members related to our congregation due to the Coronavirus. My prayers have been with the family.

I pray that if you are reading this epilogue right now (which most persons do not), many blessings and much prosperity will fill you at a capacity that you will not have enough room to contain it all. I pray for the salvation of any loved ones and friends of yours. I pray that you will pass this book on to someone who needs it at the perfect time of their life. Amen.

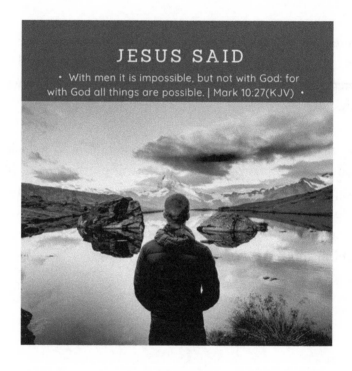

# ENDNOTES

## Introduction

Continued: Definition used from Webster's Dictionary.

## Chapter One

Urijah Faber vs. Mike Brown by Elliot Worsell
(https://www.fightersonlymag.com/features/pain-barrier-fighters-famously-fought/).

Isaiah 52:14 (New International Version).

2 Timothy 4:9-18 (The Message Translation): "Paul's insight in this letter gives us truth to the reality of relationships" by John C. Maxwell, Injoy Inc.

Acts 15:36-41 (The Message Translation).

Matthew 26:45-46 (New International Version).

## Chapter Two

Proverbs 29:11 (New King James Version).

Proverbs 15:15 (New Living Translation.

James 1:19 (The Message Translation).

A spiteful son kills four in a fit of rage by History.com (https://www.history.com/this-day-in-history/a-spiteful-son-kills-four-in-a-fit-of-rage), Publisher A&E Television Networks.

"Moses kills with Anger," *Anger: Facing the Fire Within* by June Hunt.

General Strain Theory (GST) by Scott A. Bonn Ph.D. (www.psychologytoday.com).

Anger Can Kill You If You Let It by Julie Steenhuysen.

## Chapter Three

Leviticus 15:19 (New International Version).

Ephesians 3:20 (New International Version).

2 Corinthians 1:3-4 (English Standard Version).

Philippians 4:7 (English Standard Version).

Deuteronomy 31:6 (English Standard Version).

Psalms 147:3 (English Standard Version).

1 Peter 5:7 (English Standard Version).

Isaiah 40:29 (English Standard Version).

Philippians 4:19 (English Standard Version).

Matthew 11:28 (English Standard Version).

2 Corinthians 6:18 (English Standard Version).

Thessalonians 3:3 (English Standard Version).

## Chapter Four

Galatians 5:7 (New International Version).

John 19:28-30 (New International Version).

Four vision killers and how you can stop them by Debbie McDaniel (https://www.crosswalk.com/).

## Chapter Five

Proverbs 14:4 (New International Version).

John 2:1-6 (New International Version).

Proverbs 18:19 (New Living Translation).

## Chapter Six

2 Timothy 2:3-4 (New Living Translation).

"Every thinking person wishes that armies were not necessary," paragraph by John C. Maxwell, Injoy Inc.

"The boots (shoes) of the Roman soldiers were thick, reinforced, and had a nail-studded sole," paragraph in *Sparkling Gems From the Greek Vol. 1: 365 Greek Word Studies for Every Day of the Year To Sharpen Your Understanding of God's Word* by Rick Renner.

Judges 7:3 (New International Version).

Judges 7:4-6 (New International Version).

Judges 7:7 (New International Version).

"Never Lost worship" song by Elevation Worship.

"Nepalese fighters" in *One Crowded Hour* by Tim Bowden.

"I'm going to stay on the battlefield," written by C. l. Franklin.

## Chapter Seven

Three stages of CML by Cancercenter.com (https://www.cancercenter.com/cancer-types/leukemia/stages).

"Live Like You Were Dying" song by Tim McGraw.

Luke 2:6, 7 (New International Version).

Luke 5:3 (New Living Translation).

John 6:8-11 (New International Version).

Matthew 21:1-3 (New Living Translation).

Mark 14:12-15 (New Living Translation).

Luke 23:50-56 (New Living Translation).

2 Corinthians 5:1 (New Living Translation).

Psalm 39:4 (New Living Translation).

Psalm 119:19 (New Living Translation).

1 Peter 1:17 (New Living Translation).

Philippians 3:20 (New Living Translation).

1 Peter 2:11 (New International Version).

1 Corinthians 7:31 (New International Version).

## Chapter Eight

Matthew 11:20-24 (New Living Translation).

## Chapter Nine

Romans 8:1 (New International Version).

*Doubt, Discouragement, Diversion, Defeat, Delay*: The Chronicle Life Application Study Bible.

Matthew 28:18-20 (New International Version).

Genesis 1:26 (New International Version).

Psalm 115:16 (New International Version).

Luke 10:19 (New International Version).

Matthew 16:19 (New International Version).

Romans 16:20 (King James Version).

"Suntribo," in *Sparkling Gems From the Greek Vol. 1*: 365 Greek Word Studies for Every Day of the Year To Sharpen Your Understanding of God's Word by Rick Renner.

## Chapter Ten

*"Pain is temporary. Quitting lasts forever,"* quote by Lance Armstrong.

*"Age wrinkles the body. Quitting wrinkles, the soul,"* quote by Douglas Macarthur.

"If you quit once it becomes a habit. Never quit," quote by Michael Jordan.

John 3:1-2 (New International Version).

"The Roman Government Law" by John C. Maxwell, Injoy Inc.

Matthew 5:41 (New International Version).

*Six Prominent Religions*: The Chronicle Life Application Study Bible.

*Six Reasons Why Jesus' Trial Was Illegal/Hearings*: The Chronicle Life Application Study Bible.

# ABOUT THE AUTHOR

For more than thirty years, Fernando E. Franco Sr. has been full time in the ministry. Around the whole world, Fernando E. Franco Sr. has preached, he has raised countless disciples and has been a life coach to many, including celebrities.
Currently in Oxnard, California he is the lead pastor of City—View Worship Church along with his wife Veronica Franco.

He has authored the book *dis.con.tinued* and furthermore provides growth material for leaders on his website The Online Church Growth Material.

He hosts a monthly video podcast on Facebook Live. His lessons could also be found on Apple Podcasts. He is the Founder and owner of Franco Publishing Company.

His wife Veronica and children, Fernando Franco Jr., Destiny Franco and two grandchildren Hannah Franco, Angel Borjas Jr. all reside in Oxnard, California.

Available on Amazon, Barnes & Noble, Target, Walmart, Kobu and including over 40,000…

- Independent bookstores
- Online stores
- Chain stores
- Ebook retailers
- Libraries
- Universities